How to Live—and Die—With

California Probate

Second Edition

Gulf Publishing Company
Book Division
Houston, London, Paris, Tokyo

How to Live — and Die — With

California Probate

Second Edition

Wills, Trusts, and Estate Planning in Layman's Language

Leland Alan Stark, Editor
In association with the
BEVERLY HILLS BAR ASSOCIATION

How to Live—and Die—With

California Probate

Second Edition

Library of Congress Cataloging in Publication Data

Stark, Leland Alan.
How to Live—and Die—With California Probate
Includes index.
1. Probate law and practice-California-Popular works. 2. Inheritance and succession—California—Popular works. I. Title. II. Title: Wills, trusts, and probate.
KFC205.Z9S8 1984 346.79405'2 83-22863
ISBN 0-87201-095-3 347.940652

Acknowledgments

The Beverly Hills Bar Association sincerely thanks the Bar Association of San Francisco and the State Bar of Texas for consenting to the preparation of this second edition. Special gratitude is expressed for the very fine work done on the first edition by the nineteen distinguished San Francisco lawyers and Harold I. Boucher, who served as editor. Special thanks is also due to Charles A. Saunders, editor of the original Texas book, for his helpful guidance.

The authors of this second edition were selected for their special expertise and clarity of expression and include members of the Probate, Trust and Estate Planning Section as well as the Taxation Section of the Beverly Hills Bar Association. The authors and the chapters they contributed in this new edition are as follows:

Chapter	Author(s)*
1	Gary M. Ruttenberg
2	Kenneth A. Feinfield
3	Jonathan A. Karp
4	James L. Pocrass and Nina Madden Sabban
5	Lance M. Weagant and Kathryn A. Ballsun
6	Kenneth A. Feinfield and Kathryn A. Ballsun

* Biographical information on each of these authors appears following the glossary.

7	Gary M. Ruttenberg
8	Kenneth A. Feinfield
9	Kenneth A. Feinfield and Gary M. Ruttenberg
10	Victor E. Portanova
11	Douglas K. Freeman and Gary Stern
12	Myron Siedorf
13	Gary Stern
14	Gary Stern and Douglas K. Freeman
15	Lance M. Weagant
16	Douglas K. Freeman
17	Irving Kellogg
18	Irving Kellogg and Victor E. Portanova
19	Regina I. Covitt and Lance M. Weagant
20	Lance M. Weagant

I owe a special debt of gratitude to Mildred Eleanor Haft who tirelessly read drafts of each chapter and made many valuable suggestions.

I am very grateful to my capable legal assistant, Sharron Callender Craig, for typing the drafts of this book and coordinating its compilation with her usual cheerful competence.

I would also like to thank attorneys Bruce S. Ross, Robert E. Bennett, Richard D. K. Josslin, and Terence S. Nunan; and Phyllis Cardoza, independent legal assistant, for reviewing the manuscript for changes effective in 1984 to the California Probate Code and for other helpful suggestions.

I would also like to acknowledge the extra efforts of Bill Lowe and his assistant, Melissa Lewis, of Gulf Publishing Company for their special expertise and guidance.

Leland Alan Stark, Editor

Contents

Preface

Protecting your family while saving them money, taxes, and avoidable costs at death requires careful planning. Yet often the information available is too technical for the lay person to understand. To meet the need for an introduction to estate planning that can be easily understood, the Beverly Hills Bar Association undertook the publication of this book. This fully up-to-date second edition is the work of California lawyers for Californians and those with property in California.

The first edition was prepared in 1970 by the Bar Association of San Francisco and was based on a similar book by the Real Estate, Probate and Trust Law Section of the State Bar of Texas entitled *How to Live—And Die—With Texas Probate*.

You'll be surprised to learn the taxes and costs your family will have to pay if you don't plan. And you'll be delighted to learn how these taxes and costs can be substantially reduced, if not entirely eliminated, through proper planning.

Community property, probate, and new alternatives now available under recent changes in the law are described in detail along with many different ways of handling property on death. Planning opportunities and their advantages and disadvantages are clearly pointed out. You'll also read about the various types of trusts and learn which ones can save you money as well as protect your loved ones. Finally, you'll become aware of the pitfalls in a homemade will and the solutions to some of the problems presented by ownership of a business or farm.

This book is not intended to be a do-it-yourself substitute for carefully made estate plans. Indeed, today it is only the foolhardy who attempt such a substitute. On the contrary, it is intended to alert you to some of the problems your family will face if you do not plan, and the many alternatives available with professional guidance.

General principles have been stated to provide an overall view of the subject. The reader with expertise will observe that certain exceptions to general rules have been omitted. Thus, the importance of personal consultation with the family lawyer proficient in the field of estate planning cannot be stressed enough.

Adley M. Shulman
President,
Beverly Hills Bar Association

Bruce D. Sires
Chairman,
Probate, Trust and Estate
Planning Section

Robert S. Ogilvie
Chairman,
Taxation Section

Leland Alan Stark
Editor

1
What Is Probate?

The law of probate—the law of dealing with the transmission of property from a decedent to his beneficiaries—is centuries old, yet little understood. The purpose of probate, the people it protects, and the advantages it offers should be understood by the man in the street, and with this understanding he should be moved to plan his estate to achieve probate's highest purposes, protections, and advantages.

The original meaning of the word *probate* was "to test and to prove." This word has come to mean the procedure for establishing an instrument as the last will and for doing all those things that the probate court has jurisdiction to do in settling estates.

Probate proceedings involve determining whether the deceased left a valid will and whether a will should be admitted to probate. A personal representative for the estate is qualified and appointed. This representative collects the assets, pays valid claims, and may sell property to pay debts and death taxes. The proceedings determine those entitled to receive the property, distribute their property to them, and settle the accounts of the personal representative. The representative is discharged, the sureties are released from their bond, and the estate is closed.

What Is a Personal Representative?

The personal representative of the decedent's estate is the person appointed by the court to act for the estate. This person qualifies by taking an oath and posting a bond if one is required. Individuals, banks, and trust companies may act in this capacity. The personal representative is known as the *executor* if specifically named in the will, as the *administrator with will annexed* if not named in the will and as the *administrator* if the decedent left no valid will. The court will appoint as executor the person named in the will unless some special reason compels a different appointment.

The clerk of the court issues *letters testamentary* to an executor or *letters of administration* to an administrator after appointment by the court, the filing of the oath of office, and the posting of any required bond. These *letters* are a printed form certified by the court clerk that the holder is in charge of the estate and entitled to possession of the assets.

Many small estates are administered by the public administrator, a county official who acts if no executor has been named and no one else who is entitled by law wishes to act as administrator.

In the next chapter we will discuss the steps taken by the personal representative during probate, but now we will identify which assets are probated and which are not.

What Is the Estate?

The *estate* of a person includes everything he owns. In this sense, a person's estate is the aggregate of all his assets, riches, and fortune and includes his rights to receive income from property owned by another.

This is to be distinguished from the *probate estate*, which is only the property administered by the personal representative subject to the terms of any will and control of the court. It does not include property which does not pass into the hands of the personal representative. The *probate estate* exists until the debts have been paid, the property has been distributed and the personal representative has been discharged.

The *probate estate* is not to be confused with the *gross estate*. The *gross estate* is defined for purposes of assessing the estate tax that we will discuss in Chapter 11. A deceased person may have owned, controlled, or enjoyed income from property which is part of his *gross estate* for tax purposes but not part of his *probate estate*.

Common examples of property included in the gross estate that is not part of the probate estate are:

1. Conveyances of property in which the deceased retained the income or certain elements of control for his lifetime.

2. Trusts created by a person who retained the right to revoke, alter, or amend the trust, to control the beneficial enjoyment of the trust property, or to receive the income.

What Is Not Included in the Probate Estate?

The probate estate may not include all of the property owned by a deceased person during his lifetime. This is important to recognize, since a common misconception is that a will determines the disposition of all of a person's property. A will only directs who receives the property of the probate estate. Even a person of modest means usually owns property said to be a part of his estate which may not pass under his will and never becomes part of his probate estate. Such property may include insurance, employee benefits, social security, bonds, property in joint tenancy, and trust property. We will discuss each type separately.

Insurance

Life insurance is payable on a person's death in the manner provided by the policy. It is usually made payable to a named beneficiary, and in the case of the prior or simultaneous death of the beneficiary, it is made payable to a contingent beneficiary. The insured is usually the owner of the entire policy, or the policy is part of the community estate of the insured and his spouse. The proceeds of such policy are generally not payable to the personal representative of the estate of the insured and do not become a part of his probate estate. However, the proceeds will be a part of the probate estate of the insured if they are made payable to the estate by the terms of the policy or if all named beneficiaries die before the proceeds become payable. Moreover, if there are no named and qualified primary or contingent beneficiaries and if the insured owned the policy, the proceeds are payable to the personal representative of the estate. We will return to a discussion of insurance in Chapter 16.

Annuities and Employee Benefits

Annuities, pensions, and employee benefits usually are not included in the probate estate. An annuity may be payable under what is known as an *annuity contract* or under an insurance policy with provisions for direct payment of benefits during the lifetime of the insured and perhaps thereafter. An individual may be the beneficiary of an annuity purchased by him or purchased by another for him. He may be an employee of a corporation which has a pension plan or profit-sharing plan under which he and his family are entitled to payments. In most cases any amounts payble after the death of the beneficiary will be made according to the terms of the annuity contract, insurance policy, or pension plan. These amounts generally do not become part of the probate estate unless the estate is named as the beneficiary.

Social Security

Social Security benefits and pensions payable under federal law generally do not become part of the probate estate. However, any amounts payable prior to the death of a beneficiary are payable to the personal representative of his estate as part of the probate estate.

Bonds

United States savings bonds may be made payable to the deceased, to a co-owner, or to a beneficiary named by the decedent. If the bond is payable to a co-owner or named beneficiary who survives the deceased, the survivor becomes the absolute owner of the bonds. These bonds are not part of the decedent's probate estate, although they may be included, in whole or in part, in the gross estate for tax purposes. The United States Supreme Court has held that bonds purchased by Californians with community funds are not subject to the community property laws of California and that federal and Treasury regulations prevail over state law. An example of the consequences of this will be discussed in Chapter 19. Of course, these bonds will be part of the surviving co-owner's or named beneficiary's probate estate if he still owns them and has not caused them to be reissued to himself as a co-owner or to a named beneficiary.

Property in Joint Tenancy

Property owned by the deceased and another in joint tenancy with right of survivorship is not part of the probate estate of the deceased.

This property is often referred to as joint tenancy property. It passes to the surviving joint tenant upon the death of the deceased joint owner by operation of law and the contract entered into when the joint tenancy was established. Many stocks, bonds, bank accounts, savings and loan accounts, and other properties are owned in joint tenancy. This assumes that a joint tenancy with right of survivorship was created in a valid manner. Of course, the property may be included in the probate estate of the surviving joint tentant.

The California Supreme Court has held that under our community property system a husband and wife can create jointly owned property with community property. Joint tenancy with right of survivorship is commonly used in many states, but under the California property system where the husband and wife each own an undivided one-half interest in their community property, the need for joint tenancy is not the same as in other states. Much litigation, uncertainty and adverse tax consequences have resulted from unintentional or ill-advised conversion of community property into joint tenancy property. Our discussion of joint tenancy continues in Chapter 18.

Trust Property

Property conveyed by an individual, called a grantor, to a trustee to be administered in trust and distributed after the individual's death usually is not part of the probate estate. A person has the right to convey his property to a trustee to be held and administered in trust with the income and principal distributed as provided in the instrument. The grantor may make himself the trustee and may reserve the right to alter, amend, or revoke the trust. He may also make himself a beneficiary of the trust during his lifetime. Property in a revocable trust is not part of the probate estate but is included in the gross estate for tax purposes. How to avoid probate with a revocable living trust is discussed in Chapter 10.

If the deceased was the trustee or beneficiary of a trust created by another person or if he was entitled to receive income from or the use of property for his life, these rights would terminate upon his death. The property in which he had these rights would not be part of his probate estate, except for undistributed income payable to him or possibly other vested rights in the property at the time of his death.

Exempt Property, Homesteads, and Family Allowances

The exempt property and homestead laws provide for a place and surroundings protected from creditors for the surviving family to dwell in peace.

Until an inventory is filed in a probate proceeding and for a period of sixty days thereafter (or such other period as the court may for good cause order), the surviving spouse, whether husband or wife, and the minor children of a deceased person are entitled to remain in possession of the family dwelling, the wearing apparel of the family, the household furniture, and other property of the decedent exempt from enforcement of a money judgment. After an inventory is filed in the probate proceeding, the probate court may order that any or all of the exempt property be set apart for the surviving spouse or if there is no spouse, for the minor children and may select and set apart one homestead in real property for the use of the surviving spouse and/or minor children. Property is set apart as a homestead for only the limited period designated by the court. Subject to the homestead right, the property remains subject to administration including testate and intestate succession.

Exempt property includes household furnishings and appliances, tools and equipment of a trade, business, or profession, a portion of a decedent's unpaid wages or salary, some types of savings deposits, and some insurance proceeds. These exempt items may be withdrawn from the probate estate and, with certain exceptions, are not subject to the payment of the debts of the deceased but are part of the gross estate for tax purposes.

A family allowance may also be provided by probate court order out of the decedent's estate for the surviving spouse, minor children, and physically or mentally incapacitated dependent children, depending upon the size of the estate and the needs of the family.

Community Property/Quasi-Community Property

The surviving spouse's one-half interest in community property is not subject to probate. The surviving spouse may, however, elect to probate his or her one half to limit personal liability for the decedent's debts chargeable to the community and quasi-community property.

Community property and quasi-community property passing to the surviving spouse may be confirmed to the surviving spouse by the court without the necessity of formal probate proceedings. For a more detailed discussion on community property and quasi-community property see Chapter 19.

Summary Administration of Small Estates

Persons entitled to the estate of the deceased may be able to take possession of it without formal probate administration if the estate is small. California law provides several different procedures for collection of a decedent's assets and summary administration with the differences depending on the type of assets and the size of the estate. Our discussion of these valuable procedures appears in Chapter 8.

Summary

Not everything a person owns or considers his property will end up in his probate estate. Large parts of the estate often go to beneficiaries outside of the will. Therefore, care should be taken to make certain that a sufficient amount of property (probate estate) will pass under the will to pay estate debts, take care of legacies, and accomplish the purposes intended by the will.

2
Time Schedule for Estate Administration

The length of time necessary to have a will probated or to have an estate administered if there is no will is often the basis for complaints against probate procedures. The truth of the matter now is that California probate procedure is time consuming only if the particular circumstances warrant it. The personal representative must file a petition for final distribution or a verified report on the status of the estate within one year after issuance of *letters testamentary* if no estate tax return is due. If one is due, the petition or report must be filed within eighteen months. If the estate is still not in a position to be closed, the status report must state the reasons the estate cannot then be distributed and closed.

Within the Independent Administration of Estates Act, an executor or administrator may conduct certain aspects of estate administration more easily and many time consuming administrative steps may be saved.

Nevertheless, certain real property title transfers and the handling of certain business interests at death simply cannot be disposed of overnight.

The income tax savings arising from the use of the estate as a separate taxpayer can be quite significant. This is one of the situations where it could be disadvantageous to close and distribute an estate immediately.

Duties of the Executor

A California executor or administrator has important duties, some of which must be performed whether or not a living trust has been used by the decedent. Let's take a look at them.

When a Californian dies, the executor named in the decedent's will sees that burial instructions in the will or in a letter to the executor or funeral home are properly carried out even before the will is probated. He looks after unprotected properties such as securities, cash, jewelry, or perishable assets. He determines whether there is adequate insurance against loss. He confers with heirs and finds out whether the surviving spouse has sufficient funds to meet household expenses and whether there are any other problems that need immediate attention. He helps with the proof of death for insurance purposes and generally prepares to collect the assets of the estate, which will be his responsibility when the will is probated.

The law requires a person having custody of a will to deliver it to the executor named in the will or to the clerk of the Superior Court within thirty days of learning of the death.

The executor has an attorney file the will for probate. After giving notice by publication in a newspaper and mailing notice to the heirs and beneficiaries, he obtains his evidence of authority called *letters testamentary* to act as executor of the will. The executor now completes the task of finding out what assets are in the estate. He must locate all bank accounts and transfer them to an account in the name of the estate, leaving money in savings accounts until the next interest date if possible. He obtains custody of securities, which may or may not be transferred into his name as executor, depending on how long the estate will be in administration. He must assume authority over any business owned by the estate, and if he does not know how to run it, he must find someone who does. He must locate and actually or symbolically take possession of all other assets of the estate.

It is necessary that he not let estate property become mixed with his own property or with the property of any other person. If the decedent left a surviving spouse, the executor must segregate the separate property of the decedent and the community property from the separate property of the surviving spouse. There may be problems with assets which are scattered in different states or even in foreign countries. He collects all the money owed the estate and is empowered to compromise, abandon, or sue for collection on an estate claim. Notice to the decedent's creditors is published prior to the appointment of the executor or administrator. Creditors must file or present their claims within four months of the first issuance of letters testamentary. If the claims are approved, the executor pays them. If any are rejected, the creditor may bring a suit against the estate.

A detailed, verified inventory of the estate assets is made. The assets are designated as community or separate property. Commissions and fees for the probate estate are based on the value of the assets. We will discuss the calculation of these commissions and fees in Chapter 9. The probate referee of the county of the Superior Court having jurisdiction will determine the value of the non-cash assets of the estate, but the executor must review these values to insure their fairness.

The executor estimates how much cash is needed to pay funeral bills, medical bills, and current bills as well as taxes and administration expenses. He provides for specific cash legacies that may be left by the will. If it is necessary to liquidate any assets to provide funds for payment of debts and cash gifts, then the executor must see to that also.

He estimates, provides for, and pays the personal income taxes due for the portion of the year that has elapsed prior to the decedent's death. He also takes care of the estate's income taxes, since the estate is a separate income taxpayer from the decedent. He prepares and files the federal and state estate tax returns if they are due.

The executor must keep detailed records of all his operations to be sure everything is done properly. He collects the income as it comes in and carefully watches investments so that appropriate action can be taken to protect estate values. For example, if the price of a stock held by the estate falls rapidly, he may sell it.

At the end of the period of administration, he distributes the estate in accordance with the will while determining the timing of distributions to beneficiaries for income tax purposes. If the will calls for the setting up of trusts, the executor may determine when and to what extent trusts are set up. If he handles this properly, important tax savings can be achieved.

After distribution of the estate has been effected and all other disbursements are properly made, the period of his administration is over. He must, of course, depend on good legal advice in all these matters, but the responsibility is ultimately his.

Time Sequence of Administration

Proving the Will

With this brief outline of the duties of an executor or an administrator in mind, a timetable of the events of probate is more easily understood.

In the typical case, the family will make an effort to locate a will immediately after death in order to be sure that there are no specific instructions dealing with burial. If there are such instructions, they need to be carried out at once. The will is then delivered to a lawyer to be filed promptly for probate. A court hearing on the petition for probate is then set.

The only delay at this point is in collecting the necessary names, addresses and ages of the beneficiaries named in the will as well as of the decedent's heirs had he died without a will. Other facts concerning the decedent (date of death, age, marital history, children's birthdays) are usually readily available.

Notice of the filing of the petition for probate of a will is typically given to all persons concerned by publishing it in advance of the hearing in a local newspaper and mailing it to each beneficiary and heir. In the petition, it is proved to the court that the decedent is dead, that he lived within the county, and that the will was properly executed according to California law. It is usually not necessary for anyone to appear at the court hearing unless someone objects to admission of the will to probate. An order is then entered by the court probating (proving) the will. At the same time, or immediately thereafter, the executor named in the will executes his oath to perform his duties and posts any required bond. Letters testamentary are then issued to him. The period of administration has begun.

The total elasped time to this point is two to four weeks, depending upon how quickly the initial information was assembled and the congestion of the particular county's Superior Court.

Collecting and Valuing Property

Immediately after qualifying, the executor begins the process of collecting and identifying the assets. The time involved here depends on the nature and complexity of the estate. If there are few assets and no claims of consequence, the process of identifying the assets is simple. However, the assets must be evaluated for tax and also probate purposes. This valuation may or may not consume an appreciable amount of time depending on the kind and quantity of the assets involved and whether expert appraisal is necessary. If there is *tangible* personal property having substantial value such as jewelry, antiques, or paintings, it is customary to obtain an expert appraisal and to furnish this to the probate referee. In effect, both the executor and probate referee agree that the expert appraisal is correct. This is usually done rapidly by professionals. Real estate appraisals, on the other hand, generally take longer. If the value of the real estate is very substantial or very doubtful, the executor may wish to obtain an expert appraisal as a check on the probate referee's valuation.

An appreciation of the process of real estate appraisal also aids in understanding the amount of time required. Property in the same general category (commercial, residential, etc.) will have the same general characteristics, and property sales may be comparable. It takes time for real estate information to be assembled, sorted, and evaluated for sound valuation. The appraisal problem involved may be that no sale of the estate property is contemplated. Instead, to establish the fair market value of that property, it is necessary to answer the hypothetical question: At the date of the decedent's death, what would a buyer be willing to pay a seller who was willing to sell in an "arms-length" business transaction? While the answer is a matter of opinion, it should have some rational basis which can be documented and made a part of the appraisal.

Another kind of property which requires time to value is closely held stock. If the stock in the estate is a listed stock on which market quotations appear daily, valuation is simple. Comparable sales are available immediately. However, stock in a family corporation presents a much more complex problem. There may not have been a sale for many years, and any sales that have occurred may not be representative because of special surrounding circumstances. In this case, valuation takes time unless there is a properly drafted buy-sell agreement to set the value. The benefits of a buy-sell agreement are discussed in Chapter 20.

Of course, if the decedent leaves a detailed list of assets accompanied by much of the necessary data for appraisal purposes, the job of the executor is simplified and shortened.

Claims of Creditors

The executor may take a reasonable time to pay the claims of the estate. If the claims are few, uncomplicated, and monetarily insignificant, payment can be made rapidly and the estate readied for distribution to the beneficiaries. If litigation arises or if the validity of the claims is disputed, the executor has adequate opportunity, subject to the court's approval, to dispose of those matters in the sensible, normal way that the decedent could have done had he lived.

Under the California statutes, the claims of creditors may be presented at any time within four months from the date of the first issuance of letters testamentary (or letters of administration if there is no will) which are usually issued immediately after the court's order admitting the will to probate. Executors sometimes dispense with the filing of creditors' claims for small bills when their validity is not in doubt. Nevertheless, it may be prudent to require creditors' claims for all bills, particularly to insure their deductibility for tax purposes.

A bond may be required to be filed with the court to protect creditors, if distributions to beneficiaries are made between two and four months from the date letters are issued. As will be discussed later, however, few estates are distributed at the earliest possible time, because of the effect of the tax laws on the timing of distributions.

Accounting and Distribution

As soon as taxes and debts have been provided for, the executor is ready to make distribution to the beneficiaries under the will. If there is a possibility of additional tax liability, a reserve for such taxes may be withheld to be distributed at such time as the taxes are finally determined. Unless the beneficiaries waive the filing of the executor's accounting, a final account must be prepared in formal terms to be filed with the court. Interim accounts may also be filed if the period of administration is long. Notice must be posted and given to anyone who has requested special notice, affording such person an opportunity to question the account in court, and a court order approving the account and directing the distribution must be obtained. This is followed by the distribution itself, the filing of beneficiaries' receipts, and an order from the court discharging the executor or administrator.

The Impact of Taxes

Federal Estate Tax

The chief reasons for a lengthy probate administration are the requirements of the federal tax laws rather than the periods set up for performing acts of administration under the probate laws.

If an estate tax return is required, it is due within nine months from the date of death. This extended period stems from the federal tax law permitting an estate to be valued either at the date of death or six months later. The executor has the option of computing and paying tax at the lower of the two values. In some cases the higher value may be chosen to achieve an increase in the basis for depreciation and for income tax purposes.

Ever since the option was first granted during the Depression, it has been desirable to delay winding up the estate to review the value six months after death. Appraisals may have to be made twice, once at the date of death and again in six months. Little, if any, extra time or expense is required for making the second valuation since most of the work will have been done in the date-of-death appraisal. It is also advantageous to pay the estate tax as late as possible, i.e., immediately before the nine-month deadline, so that the estate receives interest on the amount of the tax in the meantime. In a complex estate, one may be able to obtain an extension of time to prepare and file the return and one or more extensions to pay the estate tax. Since the estate tax return can be subject to audit by the Internal Revenue Service, the period of administration may be prolonged further. Also, the substantial estate is more likely to have assets qualifying for the deferred payment of tax in annual installments as will be discussed in Chapter 20.

Income Tax

The federal income tax may also prompt an extension of the administration period. For federal income tax purposes, the estate—which comes into being at the moment of death—is a separate taxpayer with a separate applicable tax bracket. During the period the estate exists, it provides a separate pocket into which income may be placed and on which federal income tax may be payable at a lower bracket than for either the decedent or the beneficiaries. If the tax bracket applicable to the beneficiaries is higher than that applicable to the estate, it will benefit the beneficiaries to maintain the estate as a taxpayer for as long as permissible under federal law.

It is probable that estates which remain open for two to five years or more are kept open mainly for federal tax reasons rather than for delinquency or mismanagement on the part of executors, lawyers, judges, or probate referees. The simple truth is that an executor who does his job thoroughly will not close the estate so long as it is in the best interests of the beneficiaries to keep it open, assuming that he has operated within the rules laid down by the Internal Revenue Service and the courts.

Planning by the decedent in advance, and by the executor subsequently, can indicate whether keeping the estate open for a substantial period is of advantage to the beneficiaries.

In the final analysis, if a proper will is drawn naming a competent executor, the paperwork steps will not be the time-consuming factor. The real delay will be prompted by the federal tax laws assuming the estate is not involved in any lawsuits or disputes with creditors or beneficiaries.

3
How Will My Debts Be Paid?

In the course of a lifetime every person creates debts. The size and nature of these obligations vary with individual and family situations. It is not surprising that the biggest debts usually are created by the wealthiest people since they have the assets, collateral, and credit rating to support larger borrowing. Unfortunately, many families of average means obligate themselves beyond their ability to pay thereby causing financial problems during life and most certainly after death. The biggest obligation is usually the mortgage or deed of trust on the home. In addition, there may be innumerable time payments for cars, appliances, credit cards, and other items. In any event, these obligations may become a factor to deal with in the administration of an estate.

In light of current economic conditions both spouses probably work, and both salaries are probably required to meet the monthly financial obligations. Take the case of a husband and wife with minor children. If both spouses continue to work until retirement, the mortgage on the home will normally be paid off along with most other items purchased on credit. But what if the primary wage earner dies unexpectedly at an early age? The non-employed or lower earning spouse must now support the minor children and pay the financial obligations alone. The main source of income—the primary wage earner's earning capacity—is gone. Unless the surviving spouse has sufficient earning capacity, the family will suffer a financial hardship. Therefore, it is the wise person who provides protection for the family in the event of his untimely death. This is true whether the primary source of income is the husband or wife.

Provisions in the Will

Many wills provide for the executor to pay debts, taxes, and the costs of administration. Whether or not the will so provides, the executor is under a general duty to pay obligations of the decedent's estate.

California provides rules concerning the priority for the payment of claims against the estate. Thus, for example, the following expenses have priority in the order stated: expenses of administration, funeral expenses, expenses of last illness, and family allowances to certain surviving members of the decedent's family.

The liability of the decedent's property for the debts of the decedent and the surviving spouse depends on when the debt was incurred and the reason for the debt. Thus, for example, a decedent's separate property and earnings during marriage are not subject to the debts of the surviving spouse incurred prior to the marriage. Also, a decedent's separate property is not generally liable for the debts of the surviving spouse other than for the necessities of life. However, the decedent's separate property is subject to all his own debts. Community property is generally liable for debts incurred by either spouse, except for funeral expenses and the expenses of last illness which are payable out of the estate of the decedent and are not charged to the community share of the surviving spouse.

In the event the community property of a decedent is liable for any debts, the decedent's share of the community property may be liable for the full amount of the debt, notwithstanding the debt having been incurred by the surviving spouse or the surviving spouse's share of the community property being equally liable for the debt. However, the representative of the decedent's estate may petition the court for an order allocating responsibility for payment of the debt between the decedent's and surviving spouse's shares of the community property. Thus, for normal family expenses incurred during marriage, the surviving spouse's share of the community property can be held liable for one half of the amount of the debt.

In the event the testator desires the assets in the estate to be fully liable for the debt and the surviving spouse to be relieved from liability for the debt, a direction in the will to that effect is essential. This is particularly important when the testator leaves property to someone other than his spouse. Moreover, the surviving spouse may mitigate her personal liability for certain debts of the decedent by probating her half of the community and quasi-community property. The scope of this liability and this probate decision must be carefully reviewed with counsel.

Care must be taken when including will provisions requiring the payment of debts because ambiguities can cause confusion, delays, and unnecessary expense. For example, prior to 1985 the phrase "my just debts be paid" would not ordinarily, but could be interpreted to, require the executor to pay off installment debts and long-term mortgage obligations immediately. There is also the possibility that a direction in a will that all debts be paid may operate to revive debts which have been barred by the statute of limitations. These dangers may be avoided by either providing that the executor not be required to pay debts prior to maturity but may extend or renew any debt upon such terms and for such time as he deems best or by intentionally omitting any direction in the will to pay debts. The statutes of California are effective in the ordinary situation to require all existing and matured debts to be paid in an orderly fashion.

The will should be tailored to the testator's own situation and should state the testator's intentions regarding payment of debts if the statutory scheme is inappropriate. For example, does the testator wish the home to pass to the surviving spouse burdened with the mortgage or with the mortgage paid if there are assets to satisfy the mortgage? In any event you should consult an attorney about the final effect of changes set for January 1, 1985.

Funeral Expenses

Occasionally a testator will include detailed funeral arrangements in his will. If the testator feels strongly about some special funeral arrangements, he should also communicate his feelings to a member of the family because the will is often not readily accessible at the time of death.

Funeral expenses and related items such as tombstones, grave markers, crypts, or burial plots are chargeable against the estate of the decedent but not the community share of the surviving spouse. As a matter of public policy, such expenses are granted a high priority for payment. If the testator does not have burial insurance and if the will does not otherwise provide for their payment, funeral expenses will be paid out of such assets as are available in the estate. Depending upon the employment history, marital status, and age of surviving children, the decedent's estate may be entitled to reimbursement of a portion of the funeral expenses from the Social Security Administration. If prior arrangements have not been made, emotional factors at the time of death may cause excessive funeral expenses.

Estate Taxes

The estate taxes may well be, and in many instances are, the largest cost chargeable to the estate.

It is the obligation of the executor to pay such taxes as are due. Here again, the testator may have made provisions to satisfy death taxes. If not, then the executor must look first to any available cash. If there is none or if the cash is insufficient, then liquid assets, such as stocks and bonds, must be sold to provide the necessary funds. Failure to provide funds for the payment of taxes may defeat the effect of will provisions for the beneficiaries.

Many people do not have much cash but are wealthy "on paper." That is, they own illiquid assets which have substantially appreciated in value since acquisition such as a closely held business or real estate. The decedent may wish to leave these assets to the surviving spouse or children or both. If upon death a significant amount of tax is due, the only alternative may be to sell all or a portion of the assets at a sacrifice price to raise the necessary funds. Certain provisions of the Internal Revenue Code may provide relief from the immediate payment of taxes, but as always, advance planning is vital to make sure the estate qualifies for the appropriate relief. Our discussion returns to these relief provisions in Chapters 11 and 20.

The situation may arise where the decedent left a will with no special direction to pay the death taxes and other costs but requested that certain assets go to certain people. For example, the home, personal effects, and life insurance proceeds go to the wife, the farm or ranch to the sons, and the stocks and bonds to the daughters. Does the testator intend the assets to pass free of taxes or bear their proportionate share of the death taxes? The will should be clear and explicit with respect to the intention. Under California law, if the will does not clearly direct the payment of death taxes out of the residue of the estate or some other specific source, then each person receiving something from the decedent pays his proportionate share of the death taxes.

Some testators wish the full amount of insurance to pass to named beneficiaries. In these instances, it is well to provide in the will that no taxes are to be charged against these policies of insurance or the proceeds of such policies.

Planning for the Payment of Debts and Taxes

There are steps that may be taken to minimize probate costs, provide for the payment of debts, and reduce estate taxes. A few important suggestions are listed here followed by the chapters where they are discussed.

1. A current will and trust, expertly drafted, may clarify many of the problems, and in addition, effect substantial tax savings. (See Chapters 6 and 13.)
2. A buy-sell agreement funded with life insurance is usually ideal when you are a member of a partnership or a closely held business. (See Chapter 20.)
3. A "mortgage insurance" policy on your home assures the home's remaining intact.
4. Sufficient life insurance pays all or some of your debts, costs of probate, and taxes. (See Chapter 16.)
5. Investments in other liquid assets that are readily marketable, such as stocks, bonds and savings accounts, can provide necessary immediate cash.
6. Endowment insurance on your children, designed to mature at the time they are ready for college, will insure future security.
7. Gifts to your children or grandchildren, directly or through trusts, give assets to those for whom you ultimately wanted to provide. Gifts may also effect substantial tax savings, since the value of gifts will generally shift the future appreciation in value of the gifted property out of the estate. (See Chapter 15.)
8. A consistent program of saving also insures future security.
9. Your careful selection of an executor with knowledge, skill, permanency, and financial responsibility is sometimes necessary

because of the complicated nature of many estates. (See Chapter 7.)

10. Contracting during lifetime for only those obligations that can be paid without financial strain minimizes after-death indebtedness.
11. Consideration of an educational, religious, or other charitable institution as the ultimate beneficiary of the estate is particularly appropriate for a family without children. Even though your survivor may have the benefit of your estate for life, if title rests ultimately in a charity, tax savings may be substantial since gifts to charity are tax deductible. The tax saving benefits of a charitable lead or remainder trust should be explored. (See Chapter 14.)

Before embarking on any one or a combination of these suggestions as a part of your formal estate plan, the advice of competent counsel should be sought.

Summary

An unavoidable fact of our existence is death, debts, and taxes. How debts and taxes are paid after death varies in direct proportion to the thought and planning given to them before death. A person who does not take advantage of the wealth of professional estate planning talent available today is indeed unwise. Procrastination may result in a decision that in time may prove very costly and bring with it a host of unwelcome surprises.

There is no substitute for competent legal advice. Home-drawn or do-it-yourself wills usually cause endless litigation and penalize the family with higher costs and increased taxes. One improper sentence in a will may cause the entire estate to be subject to tax and thus destroy the great tax advantages that are legally available with a proper estate plan.

The fee for an attorney to prepare a will which makes appropriate provision for payment of debts or does not operate to complicate the payment of such debts is small compared to the savings effected and the costly delays avoided, not to mention the potential savings in estate taxes.

4
Should I Make a Will?

Most people work hard to acquire and keep property during their lifetimes. However, a surprisingly large number of people die without a will. Those people forfeit their right to determine the disposition of their property and fail to provide for their family's continuing well-being. They die leaving the security of their family to chance and the disposition of their property to people they may not have wanted to receive it.

Who Can and Should Make a Will?

Most of the persons who die with a will are owners of at least modest or medium-sized estates. Yet the value of careful planning with professional guidance for families with smaller estates cannot be overemphasized. The smaller estate can ill afford to incur costs that could be saved for the family.

A will is a written instrument by which a person (called a testator) disposes of property at his death. It is always subject to change during his lifetime. It conveys no present interest in property nor rights to any beneficiary until the testator's death. As a result, a will can dispose of property acquired after the will was made.

California law gives to every person of sound mind who is at least eighteen years of age the right to make a will. This right carries with it the privilege of disposing of one's estate to anyone in any manner. California law does not require a will to leave property to one's spouse, children, parents, or to any other person.

Types of Wills

A *formal will* prepared by an attorney is the most common type. For such a will to be valid, it must be in writing and signed by the testator or by someone signing for him at his direction and in his presence. This form of will must be attested by at least two witnesses who sign their names at the end of the will in the presence of each other and of the person making the will who declares to them that the document is his will and requests them to witness it. If a testator does not sign the will in the presence of the attesting witnesses, he must later acknowledge in the presence of the attesting witnesses that the prior subscription was made by him or by his authority.

A witness should not be a beneficiary under the will. Consult counsel for changes effective after 1984. If the requirements for execution of the will and its attestation are not strictly complied with, the will is invalid. Likewise, if the testator is not of sound mind or is acting under undue influence when the will is executed, it is invalid. Hence, it is advisable to have an attorney supervise the making and execution of a will to assure all of the prerequisites for validity and the various formalities of execution are satisfied.

Another type of will in California is one where the signature and the material provisions are in the handwriting of the testator. This is a *holographic will* and does not require witnesses in order to be valid. We will discuss this will more in the next chapter.

California now has what is known as the *statutory will.* It begins with the following caveat—*It may be in your best interest to consult with a California lawyer because this statutory will has serious legal effects on your family and property.* It is not designed to reduce death taxes nor any other taxes. The definitions, particularly of children, should be examined to avoid unexpected beneficiaries. The *statutory will with trust* distributes all of the property to the children when the youngest is twenty-one. No changes in any words are permitted on the face of the form used for the statutory will. Both the family and economic consequences should be discussed with counsel prior to its use.

One popular misconception holds that if one has a will one may avoid probate. A will is not a probate avoidance device.

Consideration should be given to the executor's commissions and the attorney fees that result from probate of a will be it holographic, formal, or statutory. In Chapter 9 we will discuss how to calculate these commissions and fees. In Chapter 10 we will discuss how you can save the cost of probate; however, the benefits and costs of probate should be weighed, as they vary from case to case.

Dying Without a Will

If you die in California without a will, the laws of succession determine who shall inherit your property and in what proportions your property shall be distributed. These laws also govern the distribution of property not disposed of by your will, either because the will does not cover all of the property or because it is invalid. Where there is a will, unless a contrary intention is plainly expressed or necessarily implied, it will be presumed that you intended to dispose of your entire estate according to its terms.

The properties disposed of by your will, or by the laws of succession, are only your separate property and your half interest of the community property. Under the laws of succession, the dispositions of community and separate property differ. Table 4-1 shows how property not disposed of by a will is distributed to the heirs in California.

This illustrated distribution of property is the will that the State of California has written for a person who does not take the opportunity to make his own. It is inflexible and does not take into account the individual needs and requirements of the various family members. For example, if a father owning only community property dies without a will, his wife inherits everything and his children inherit nothing.

Conversely, if a father owning only separate property dies without a will, his wife will receive one half of the property if there is only one child or the lawful issue of a deceased child living and only a third of the property if there is more than one child living or one child and the lawful issue of one or more deceased children living. This is hardly the disposition the owner of a modest or medium-sized estate wants in order to protect the best interests of his wife and children. Yet, this is his will unless he does something about it.

When a parent is survived by minor children, the problems presented by dying without a will are particularly acute. The surviving spouse is obligated to support the children and often is required to do so out of his own property and earnings, even though the children may have substan-

Table 4-1
Intestate Succession*

A MAN DIES LEAVING ↓ / TYPE OF PROPERTY → / HIS PROPERTY, IF HE MAKES NO WILL, GOES TO →	COMMUNITY					SEPARATE				
	HIS WIFE	HIS ONLY CHILD	HIS CHILDREN	HIS PARENT OR PARENTS	HIS BROTHERS AND SISTERS	HIS WIFE	HIS ONLY CHILD	HIS CHILDREN	HIS PARENT OR PARENTS	HIS BROTHERS AND SISTERS
Wife and Child	All	None		None	None	Half	Half		None	None
Wife and Children	All		None	None	None	One-Third		Two-Thirds	None	None
Wife No Children But Parents	All			None	None	Half			Half	None
Wife No Children No Parents	All				None	Half				Half
Wife No Children No Immediate Family	All					All				
No Wife But Children	NO COMMUNITY PROPERTY							All	None	None
No Wife No Children But Parents	NO COMMUNITY PROPERTY								All	
No Wife No Children No Parents	NO COMMUNITY PROPERTY									All
No Wife No Children	(Property from a Predeceased Spouse) SEE PROBATE CODE SECTION 229					SEE PROBATE CODE SECTION 230				

* Note: From the Trust Department, Bank of America. Not subject to the copyright of this book. Portions of this table are scheduled for change on January 1, 1985. Consult your attorney for information on the effects on your estate.

tial inheritances of their own. Where a minor receives property through inheritance, it is often necessary to have a guardian appointed not only to protect the property and the minor's rights but because the law may require a guardian before distribution can be made. Insurance companies and governmental agencies, such as the Social Security Administration and the Veterans Administration, require a guardianship before they will pay funds to a minor beneficiary. When a minor inherits an interest in real estate, title companies and lending agencies may require that a guardianship be established before the minor's interest can be sold.

Guardianship—Penalty of Dying Without a Will

The administration of the minor's property under a guardianship is highly restricted and subject to court supervision to safeguard the minor's rights. The minor's money can be invested only in authorized investments, and the guardian's expenditures are also regulated. At age eighteen his property must be delivered to him, regardless of his maturity or business experience.

One of the unique advantages of making a will is the opportunity for the parent or grandparent to establish a trust to administer the minor's property. The trust will avoid the necessity of a guardianship, and the parent or grandparent can prescribe in the trust his own rules for the management of the trust funds, how and for what purposes the money is to be spent, and who is to be the trustee. The trust can continue after the child becomes eighteen so that he can mature and gain experience in the management of property before it is distributed to him. Further, the final distribution need not be all at once but can be made in installments, enabling the child to assume responsibility in stages. In addition; the trust can provide who receives the property if the child dies before final distribution.

Dying Without a Will—Who Handles the Estate?

If there is no will naming a personal representative to handle the administration of the decedent's estate, California law provides a list of persons with priorities from which the court will select one individual. The duties of the personal representative (called an *administrator* if there is no will) are to locate all of the property of the decedent, take the property into his possession, collect all debts due the estate, manage it during the period of administration, pay the debts, taxes, and costs of administration, and distribute what is left according to the laws of succession. The administrator may or may not be the person the decedent would have selected for this responsibility. It may not be the surviving spouse or even a member of the decedent's family, and it might even be a creditor or the public administrator. By making a will, the testator can choose the person he wants to be his personal representative and can decide which persons are going to receive his property.

Wife Should Have a Will

It is as important for the wife to have a will as it is for the husband. Since most property owned by married people in California is community property, the wife usually owns half of the family wealth. Where there is no will, the wife's community property may pass outright to an already wealthy husband and sacrifice a very significant tax benefit on the husband's later death. See Chapter 13 on the bypass trust. The husband's will alone does only half the job of planning for the family.

Dying With an Out-Dated Will

California law makes a special provision for children born or adopted either before or after the execution of a will by their parent. When a decedent omits to provide in his will for any child or issue of a deceased child, whether born before or after the making of the will, such child or issue succeeds as if there had been no will unless:

1. Provision was made by a settlement.
2. An equal proportion of the testator's property was given him as an advancement.
3. It appears from the will that such omission was intentional.

The statutes are not intended as a limitation upon the testator's powers; he may intentionally disinherit any child or issue. The purpose is to protect against his forgetfulness as well as to take care of children born after the making of the will.

Marriage and Divorce—Their Effect on a Will

A divorce by the testator does affect the provisions of his will if the testator and his former spouse have executed a property settlement agreement waiving rights to inherit the other's estate and the will is executed on or after January 1, 1981. Otherwise, prior to January 1, 1985, the divorce does not eliminate from the will of each divorced spouse all provisons affecting the other spouse. For example, suppose a man makes a will leaving a portion of his estate to his wife. Then the man and wife are divorced with no waiver in a property settlement agreement, and the man dies before remarrying and updating his will. The portion of the estate he designated to go to the wife will still pass to her, regardless of their divorce. Counsel should be consulted as to the final effect of changes set for January 1, 1985.

However, where the testator remarries subsequent to execution of his will, the new wife receives what she would have received had there been no will unless the will or an agreement signed by the spouses provides for the new wife or indicates a specific intention not to provide for her.

Everyone Should Have an Up-to-Date Will

Even though a person has a properly drawn will that is kept in a place where it can be found at his death, it will be of little value to the beneficiaries if it is not up-to-date. Parenthood, grandparenthood, divorce, changing needs of beneficiaries, change of residence, sale of property mentioned in the will, unavailability of an executor or trustee, gifts, newly acquired assets, changes in the laws, and a change in the size of the estate are all indications that the will needs to be reviewed by the testator's lawyer. An out-of-date will that no longer fits your desires or the needs of your beneficiaries is little better than no will at all.

The introduction of the new unlimited marital deduction has made many wills out of date. The special requirement to amend these wills to receive this new benefit is described in Chapter 13.

Dying without a will rarely, if ever, provides a satisfactory substitute for the making of a will. Without a will you have no choice as to who will administer your estate, who will be the guardian of your minor children, or who will receive your property, in what proportions, and when. A will assures you that your property goes to the persons you want it to and in the manner you desire. You can name an executor of your will, a guardian for your children, and a trustee. As we discussed in the last chapter, a will also allows you to choose the sources from which debts, expenses of administration, and taxes are to be paid. Further, it can save money in court costs, guardian fees, and attorney fees. But even more important are the savings to your family in time and worry and the assurance to them that you planned for their continued well-being. A will, very often, is the most important legal document that you will ever execute. It, therefore, deserves thoughtful consideration and skillful preparation.

Summary

A carefully prepared will containing all of the provisions necessary to transmit your property to those you want to receive it can be a real legacy in itself. Such a will relieves the surviving family of the many problems created by a will improperly prepared or no will at all. It seems, then, that each thoughtful man and woman owes a duty to his or her family to have a carefully prepared will in keeping with present family circumstances.

5
Pitfalls of a Homemade Will

Many people ask, "Do I need a lawyer to draft my will?" For California residents, as well as residents in most other states, the answer is "no." However, the question still remains: "Should I draft my own will?"

Take the case of Mr. Black, a widower who decided to write his own will. At that time his only descendant was his granddaughter. Mr. Black believed that she had inherited more than enough from his wife and her parents who were killed in an airplane accident. So Mr. Black wrote his own will leaving his entire estate to certain nieces, nephews, and others. While he left his estate to designated individuals, he did not specifically mention his granddaughter in any of the several pieces of paper, all in his own handwriting, which constituted his will. However, there was absolutely no doubt that Mr. Black knew about her and that the omission to provide for her was intentional. Nevertheless, the court held that his granddaughter was a "pretermitted" heir under California law and therefore, the entire will was invalid. Accordingly, Mr. Black died intestate (without a will), and his granddaughter received all of his estate as Mr. Black's nearest blood relative. One can only wonder what Mr. Black would have thought of such a result.

The Holographic Will

As we discussed in the last chapter, a holographic will is one in which the signature and all the material provisions are in the handwriting of the testator (the person making the will). The holographic will need not be dated, as was previously the case in California. If the holographic will is not dated and there is another will with inconsistent provisions, the holographic will is invalid to the extent of the inconsistency unless the time of its signing is established to be after the date of the signing of the other, dated will. If the holographic will is undated and the testator lacked testamentary capacity at any time when it might have been signed, the holographic will is invalid unless it is proved that the holographic will was signed at a time when the testator had testamentary capacity.

Ambiguity

One of the major problems involved in a homemade will is ambiguity. Lay persons often write in such a manner that their intentions are perfectly clear to themselves, but beneficiaries, attorneys, and judges find major ambiguities which are often resolved by expensive litigation or compromise.

Here is one example sometimes found in a homemade will: "I give my wife everything I have, and upon her death, I give what is left for the benefit of my children." Problems are created by such phrasing. Does the surviving spouse get the property or only the right to use the property for life? May the surviving spouse sell, mortgage or lease the property, and if so, how may the surviving spouse invest the proceeds of the sale? What happens if the surviving spouse commingles the decedent's property with the surviving spouse's own property including what the surviving spouse may acquire after the decedent's death? Can one spouse give the property away during his or her lifetime? Ordinarily, the words "for the benefit of" create a trust. Is a trust created for the children? If a trust is created, who is the trustee, and what are the terms of the trust? When does the trust come to an end? These are merely some of the questions raised by the above example.

If a testator states, "I give $25,000 to my three sons," does he mean $25,000 to be divided among the three sons or does he mean $25,000 to each? If the testator declares, "I give all my land in Alpine County to my son," and the land is subject to a mortgage, does the son have to pay the mortgage or is it paid by the estate?

Another type of ambiguity is that involved in a gift of money on deposit in a bank. Does the statement "I leave the money on deposit at the First National Bank" mean only what was on hand when the will was made (say $1,000) or when the decedent died (say $25,000)? If it turns out that at the decedent's death there are two bank accounts, a checking account he had when he made his will and a savings account he opened later, who gets what?

Suppose a testator gives $1,000 or 10 shares of XYZ stock to Henry Smith. What does the executor do if XYZ stock is selling for $500 a share at a total value of $5,000? Does the beneficiary have his choice?

Another recurring problem is the gift of a specific number of shares of stock without a reference to stock splits or stock dividends. For example, the testator may give 100 shares of XYZ stock. Later, a stock dividend of 5 shares for each one of the original 100 shares is declared. If the provision is interpreted literally, the recipient of 100 shares would have only a fifth the number of shares which the testator may have intended.

Consider the following statement: "I give my business to my son." What happens to the accounts receivable, the inventories, the cash in the bank and other assets belonging to the business? If the business is located on a piece of land owned by the testator, who gets the land?

Advantages of Attorney-Drafted Wills

One of the real advantages of obtaining professional advice about what to put in your will is that your discussion with your lawyer will help you decide what your basic desires are, what you wish to do with your property, and what alternatives are available to you to achieve your objectives. Thus, you will more carefully consider the nature and extent of all your assets and the alternatives with which you can aid your family, friends, business associates, and charitable interests in the most economic way. You are made aware of possibilities that you have never before considered and are provided with alternative solutions and recommendations. Moreover, you are made aware of what it is going to cost your family in taxes, delays, and fees if you fail to plan. You are generally delighted to learn that the cost of planning is quite small in comparison to the amounts saved.

For example, if a testator merely wills his property to his spouse or children, the testator may fail to provide properly for the continuation of a business or the handling of a partnership interest or in some way place his family in conflict with his surviving business associates. All of these things can be specifically handled in the will and with the planning described in Chapter 20 during the testator's lifetime in a way that will protect the testator's family at his death. Often such matters are overlooked by a person making his own will or complicated by incomplete or ambiguous dispositions. Administrative provisions generally not included in homemade wills are included in attorney-drafted wills that save time and money.

Unintentional Disinheritance

If a testator prepares his own will, the testator may fail to provide for certain persons he actually wants to benefit. For example, the testator may leave property to his only son or, if the son is not living at the testator's death, to his son's children. The latter event may in fact occur, and his daughter-in-law will get nothing. However, she must raise the minor children who will get all the inheritance, and she must do it under the restrictions of a court-supervised guardianship which will continue until the children attain the age of eighteen. A guardianship would require the added expense of applications to and orders from the probate court to do various things in connection with the guardianship estate. It might further require the filing and probate court approval of periodic accounts, as well as a final accounting when each child attains his or her majority. A revocable living trust as described in Chapter 10 or a testamentary trust as described in Chapter 13 can ameliorate these problems.

Sometimes a testator writing his own will makes large bequests of money to friends or others. Such incidental bequests may leave little for the real object of his bounty because of a shrinkage in the estate or a failure to account for liabilities.

Other Significant Omissions

Many other important matters are often overlooked in the self-made will. There may be a failure to give directions to an executor as to what to do about taxes due on a life insurance policy. The estate without the insurance may be quite small, but the large insurance policy will cause the estate to have to pay an estate tax. Who should pay the tax on the insurance proceeds? Should it be the individual named in the policy or the person entitled to the residue of the estate under the will?

The self-made will may fail to designate a successor executor or trustee in the event the one originally named dies or for whatever reason decides not to serve. In the absence of the designation of a successor, the administration would have to proceed with an administrator appointed by the probate court.

Sufficient attention may not be given to the possibility of one death occurring within a short time of another. If a testator gives all of his property to a surviving spouse, all the property may go to the surviving spouse's family under her will to the complete exclusion of the testator's family, even though there may be only a few minutes difference in the times of their deaths.

Finally, the non-lawyer drafted will generally will not comply with the technical requirements for funding a *bypass trust,* which may be desirable for purposes of minimizing the estate tax on the death of the surviving spouse. Likewise, the requirements of a *qualified terminable interest property* trust must be prepared by a lawyer familiar with Federal Estate Tax law. See Chapter 13 for a discussion of the savings with these valuable trusts.

Summary

There are many reasons, more than can be adequately discussed in this chapter, why it is not advisable for a person inexperienced in legal and tax matters to attempt to draw his or her own will. Such wills constitute, and will continue to constitute, a prolific source of family disputes which may result in expensive and time-consuming litigation and greatly increased costs of probate. Perhaps the words of one of the appellate justices who decided the fate of Mr. Black's will best sum up the message of this chapter: "But, unfortunately, the testator knew just enough about probate law to think he could safely prepare his own will; by acting for himself, he saved an attorney's fee amounting to perhaps $10 and caused a loss to his intended devisees and legatees of well over $100,000."

This poem by Lord Neaves is dedicated to those seeking to avoid the lawyer's fee for preparing a will:

Ye lawyers who live upon litigants' fees,
And who need a good many to live at your ease,
Grave or gay, wise or witty, whate'er you decree,
Plain stuff or Queen's Counsel, take counsel of me.
When a festive occasion your spirit unbends,
You should never forget the Profession's best friends;
So we'll send round the wine and bright bumper fill,
To the jolly testator who makes his own will.

6 What Should My Will Contain?

A well drawn will is tailored to the individual needs and circumstances of the person, called a testator, who signs it. An ideal provision in the will of one person might be unfit, and even dangerous, if used in the will of another. Nevertheless, there are numerous standardized provisions that should be included in most wills. Likewise, there are various problems that should be considered in the drawing of any will.

Introductory Declarations

A will should set forth the name and county of residence of the testator. A new will does not revoke a prior will unless either the new will contains an express revocation or its provisions are wholly inconsistent with the prior will. The testator should state that the present document is his last will and revokes all prior wills and codicils. The will should also state the testator's marital status and in the appropriate situation, specifically name the spouse and children, living and deceased. The will should state what property is covered, and if there is both separate property and community property, it may state which property is separate and which is community.

Naming of an Executor

The executor is the person or corporation that carries out the instructions of a will, pays the debts and taxes, and protects and manages the property until it can be delivered to the beneficiaries. If a will does not name an executor, the probate court will select someone in accordance with the priorities set forth in the California Probate Code.

To avoid such a statutorily directed court appointment and to insure that your property will be handled by someone you trust, you as testator should name an executor in your will. It is wise to ask the proposed executor whether he will accept the responsibility and discuss your plans with him. It is also desirable that your will name at least one alternate executor in case your first choice is unable or unwilling to serve.

The probate court may require that the executor furnish a bond to guarantee the faithful performance of his duties. The cost of such bond will be paid out of your probate estate. Consequently, you should decide whether to avoid this cost by specifying in the will that the executor need not post a bond.

Provisions for Payment of Debts and Taxes

The various changes in the law that we discussed in Chapter 3 regarding the liability of the community property, apportionment of debts, and the administration of one or both halves of the community and quasi-community property need to be considered in planning alternative will provisions. (See also in Chapter 3 our discussion on using the phrase "my just debts be paid.")

You should also decide whether you want each person receiving a small gift from your estate to pay his share of the estate taxes or whether these taxes should be imposed upon the residue with specific gifts passing tax free. Your will should answer this question, rather than allowing the ultimate allocation of taxes to alter your plan.

Finally, it is important that the will provisions for the payment of debts and taxes be coordinated with the other documents, particularly your living trusts.

Provisions Disposing of the Property

The principal provisions in most wills are those which set forth to whom and in what manner the testator's property shall pass upon his death. In some states the law requires that a person leave a specified proportion of his property to certain close relatives, and the courts will give such property to those relatives even if the will does not so provide. California has no such requirement. In this state a testator may leave his property to anyone in a properly drafted will—relative or not—whether it is for a good reason, a bad reason, or no reason at all.

Likewise, a testator has great freedom of choice in determining how his property shall go to the persons named in his will. He can give the property outright, he can put the property in a trust, or he can give the property on condition that the person receiving it do, or refrain from doing, whatever the testator specifies. Similarly, he can provide that the person receiving the property is to enjoy it only during his lifetime (or for a certain period of time) and thereafter the property is to go to another.

There are certain technical restrictions upon a testator's power to leave his property by will. For example, he must not try to control the property beyond the limit in the Rule Against Perpetuities. He also must not direct that it be used for an unlawful purpose or for a purpose that violates "public policy." However, subject only to such limited restrictions, a testator can and should have his will written so that his property will be disposed of in the exact manner he desires. The aim of the lawyer who drafts the will is to find out what the testator wants to do with his property and then word the will so that it carries out those desires as fully as possible. Tax consequences should be kept in mind, but personal wishes should remain paramount.

Since a testator has such wide latitude in determining how the provisions of his will are to be written, only a few general comments need to be made about them. First and foremost, the will should be written so that it covers all of the testator's property. If this is not done, costly court proceedings may be necessary regarding the omitted property. To guard against any omission, a will should always contain a residuary clause, which is a catch-all provision disposing of property not disposed of in other provisions of the will.

If a testator is putting his property into a trust or is otherwise providing for its future use and enjoyment, he should be sure to consider whether he wants his home, its furnishings, his automobile, and his personal effects to be included with the other property or whether he wants his surviving spouse or some other beneficiary to have free and unrestricted ownership of those properties. Similarly, careful consideration should be given to the naming of the trustee, successor trustees, and the various powers by which the trustee will manage and control the property.

The pattern of many wills is to direct that specific pieces or categories of property or specific sums of money shall go to certain persons and then to follow up these specific bequests with a general bequest in which the rest of the property is left to others. Thus, a testator may give a shotgun to a friend, a sum of money to a faithful employee, a farm to a certain relative, and so on, with those portions of the will being followed up by a general provision giving the rest of his property to his children. Note, however, the previous discussion about allocating the tax burden.

It is also common practice for a testator to leave general categories of personal property such as jewelry, automobiles, furniture, furnishings, and personal effects to the surviving spouse or children. In such a case, where there is family harmony, some testators leave such general gifts in the will to be equally distributed at the executor's discretion.

Usually the persons who are to receive the rest of the property are the ones whom the testator is most interested in benefiting. A common danger in this type of will is that circumstances may change between the time the will is signed and the time the testator dies. As a result the will may do exactly the opposite of what the testator intended and deny benefits to the very persons whom he wished most to benefit. For example, say a testator had property worth $100,000 in 1976, when he made his will. He wanted his children to receive the largest part of his estate, so he worded his will so that 5 friends or relatives would each receive $5,000, with the rest of the estate going to the children. However, if his estate amounted to only $25,000 when he died, the $5,000 bequests would use up the entire estate. Even though the testator intended for the children to receive most of his property, they would get nothing.

Consequently, whenever a testator is thinking about making specific bequests and then leaving the bulk of his estate to those dearest to him, he should always keep in mind that decline in the value of the estate may result in its being used up by the specific bequests. One way to prevent this is to make the specific bequests in terms of fractional parts of the estate rather than in terms of a dollar amount. Thus, in the example previously cited, the testator with an original estate of $100,000 should have made the 5 specific bequests by giving each person 1/20 of the estate, instead of giving $5,000 to each. Then, when the estate had shrunk to $25,000, the 5 specific bequests together would require only $6,250 of the estate, leaving $18,750 for the children.

Provision for Alternate Dispositions of the Property

When a testator provides in his will that most of his property shall go to a certain person, it is also wise to provide for a secondary or even a tertiary beneficiary in the event that the first and second persons die before the will takes effect. Consideration should be given to the use of survivorship clauses. For example, if a primary beneficiary fails to survive the decedent for a specified time period, say sixty days, the gift passes to the next named beneficiary. Thus, in the appropriate situation, such a dispositive pattern could avoid an unnecessary probate of the gift in the estate of a primary beneficiary who survives the decedent for only a relatively short period of time.

The use of trusts in a will is common. These are discussed in Chapter 13. Many people want to make sure their property goes to their grandchildren on the death of their children rather than their in-laws. They leave the property in trust for their children for life, with the remainder given outright to their grandchildren.

Provision for Death from a Common Accident

While it is unusual for a husband and wife to be killed as the result of a common accident or under circumstances that make it difficult to determine who died first, such remote contingencies should be planned for. Since the husband's will usually provides for the wife to take some or all of his property, and vice versa, this type of accident can lead to serious problems.

Suppose a husband's will leaves all his property to his wife, with an alternate gift to his parents in the event that she dies before he does. Likewise the wife's will leaves all of her property to her husband with an alternate gift to her parents. Then, in a common accident, the husband dies first and the wife dies 40 minutes later. Immediately upon the husband's death, title to his property will go to his wife. Forty minutes later when the wife dies, title to the property goes to her parents, eliminating his family entirely.

To avoid these problems, most wills should contain a "common accident clause," consistent with good tax planning. If death results from a common accident or under other circumstances that make it difficult to determine who died first or if the spouse dies, for example, within sixty days of the testator, the common accident clause provides for the property to be disposed of as if the testator had died after the other spouse. This results in the added benefit of avoiding the costs and delays in probating property in the estates of both spouses. Sometimes it is advisable to broaden the clause so that it will cover children as well as the husband and wife.

While tax savings are secondary to family objectives, the testator should discuss with counsel whether special drafting of this simultaneous death clause to achieve estate equalization is consistent with his overall plan.

Powers for the Executor

The executor should be given powers to buy, sell, and lease estate property and probably authority to invest and re-invest the property during estate administration. Special wording should be used in the will to provide for these powers as well as others the testator might foresee as being helpful in the administration of any unusual assets or business interests.

It should be noted that, unless the will provides to the contrary, an executor may apply to the probate court for authority to administer the estate under the Independent Administration of Estates Act. The act allows the executor much more freedom and flexibility in administering the estate by providing that certain actions may be taken by the executor without prior court authorization and other specific actions may be taken after first sending an ''advice of proposed action'' to persons interested in the estate and allowing them an opportunity to object in court.

Provision for Guardianship

When the testator has minor children, the will should name a guardian should the other parent die before the will takes effect. A child over fourteen years old may select his own guardian, subject to court approval. For the guidance of the court, it is wise to name a guardian in the will, even though a child is over fourteen.

There are two types of guardians. The guardian of the person of the minor child has custody and control of the child as well as charge of his education. The guardian of the estate of the minor child has the management and control of the child's property. The testator may name the same person in his will to perform both roles or may name one person to be guardian of the person and another to be guardian of the estate. Banks and trust companies can also be considered as possible guardians of the estate but not of the person.

Many do not wish the property to be given to their children when they become eighteen and the guardianship terminates. This can be avoided with a trust for the children that would take care of them until they are mature enough to responsibly handle the property. We will discuss trusts in Chapters 10 and 13.

Required Formalities

A will must be signed by the testator himself, or someone at his direction and in his presence must sign the testator's name. Unless the will is entirely written and signed in the testator's own handwriting, it must be signed by at least two disinterested witnesses. In the usual will where the testator signs it himself, his signature is followed by a clause reciting that he declared the instrument to be his will and that the two witnesses signed the will at his request, in his presence and in the presence of each other. This clause is then followed by the signatures of the witnesses. Further, it is recommended that this attestation clause be made by the witnesses by so declaring under penalty of perjury. Thus, the will is made "self proving," and if it is uncontested, it is possible to have the will admitted to probate without having to locate the witnesses and obtain their declarations after the testator's death. You should consult an attorney about changes in these required formalities effective after 1984.

Summary

In California, you have an almost unlimited freedom in determining to whom and how your property shall go upon your death. Your will should be "tailor-made" to carry out your wishes and meet the individual needs and circumstances of your estate. However, unless certain formalities are observed and certain common problems are solved, your desires may be frustrated; the beneficiaries named in your will may get nothing or may receive an estate greatly decreased by unnecessary and costly administrative expenses, death taxes, income taxes, and litigation. In addition to containing carefully drawn provisions disposing of your property, a will should name an executor, with power to buy, sell, and lease and perhaps authority to invest and re-invest estate property.

7
Choosing the Right Executor

Selecting the right executor is one of your most important decisions. The one appointed will be your agent to carry out the wishes and desires expressed in your will. Integrity, business experience, impartiality, willingness to serve, and sound judgment should be taken into consideration when selecting an executor.

Duties and Powers

The executor's goal is to handle the estate in the very best interests of the persons who will inherit it. The executor should preserve and manage the estate and see to the payment of obligations. He should treat the assets of the estate fairly, impartially, and confidentially.

The powers given to an executor in a will may be limited to paying debts, expenses, and taxes. The powers also may be broad and include the rights of disposing of property, making a division among the beneficiaries, and operating a business. An executorship may be continued for many years, or it may be limited to a short period of time.

Certain actions are necessary in any estate where there is a will naming an executor. Within a reasonable time after the testator's death, the will is taken to the attorney representing the executor, who will file a petition for its probate. At that time the executor should know generally the nature and extent of the properties of the estate. After the petition is filed and proper notice is given, a court hearing is held in order to prove the will and admit it to probate. The executor then qualifies and secures authority from the court to act.

The executor may request the court to grant him additional powers under the Independent Administration of Estates Act, which may ease administration, so long as the will does not provide to the contrary.

The executor is responsible for ascertaining the properties left by the testator as well as his debts and obligations. He must prepare an inventory of the properties to be submitted to the probate referee appointed by the court. If there is a going business, he must supervise it. It is most important that the proper insurance be kept in force on the properties and that any rights the estate might have be kept intact. After debts have been paid including whatever taxes are due, the executor gives his final accounting and makes distributions to the beneficiaries as directed under the will.

Who Should I Choose as Executor?

The Surviving Spouse

The surviving spouse may be capable of assuming the responsibilities of the estate. Frequently, however, the spouse is untrained in the business of probate and tax problems. Under such circumstances, it may be better to appoint a bank, a trust company, a partner, another member of the family, or a trusted friend as executor. Eventually, the surviving spouse will be expected to manage his or her own affairs, but this can be done gradually as some knowledge of the problems involved is acquired. Perhaps a coexecutorship is the answer. The surviving spouse can act together with the steadying hand of one more experienced.

Banks or Trust Companies

Banks and trust companies have been granted trust powers. Their trust departments are strictly supervised by state and federal authorities. Many banks and trust companies through decades of experience have evolved systems and procedures that will protect the estate while relieving the surviving spouse of the myriad of details that would otherwise have been his responsibility as executor. Banks and trust companies may also provide the ideal neutral party if a family dispute were to arise. Their institutional nature insures longevity. As executor, a bank or trust company may employ the testator's own attorney and accountant in handling the estate. Instructions may be left either in the will or separately which may recommend an attorney and accountant. Alternatively, an individual executor may selectively employ certain banks or trust companies to perform specific tasks to ease the administration of an estate.

Compensation of an Executor

The executor is only entitled those fees allowed by law in California. The law provides that an executor shall be entitled to receive a commission computed at statutory rates upon the amount of estate accounted for by him. This statutory commission covers all ordinary services of the executor. If extraordinary services are required, the court may allow the executor additional compensation. See Chapter 9 for details. An individual, whether it is the surviving spouse, a child, or a trusted friend, although entitled to charge the same fee as any other executor, may for personal reasons charge little, if anything, other than actual expenses incurred.

An Alternate Executor

An executor must, of course, live longer than the person appointing him. It may be well, therefore, not to name someone more advanced in age than the testator. The vicissitudes of life are such that an alternate or successor executor should be named in every will with the same powers and rights as the first executor named.

As noted in Chapter 5, it is legal though not wise to attempt to draw one's own will. There are numerous pitfalls which may make that attempt to save money a most expensive mistake. This includes naming an executor without the proper expressions concerning his powers and responsibilities.

Powers of an Executor

The California Probate Code covers the powers and responsibilities of executors, but some of the statutory powers may be broadened by provisions in the will. The will can grant the executor specially drafted powers to sell and lease property of the estate, to continue a business owned by the decedent, and to invest surplus funds of the estate in a specified manner. The will can also authorize the executor to serve without bond. Unless bond is waived in the will or by all of the beneficiaries, the executor (except a bank or trust company) will be required to be bonded at additional expense to the estate.

Coexecutors

The problem of choosing the right executor may be solved by naming two or more persons as coexecutors. You may not want to name one child over another for fear of the possible friction. This problem may be solved by naming two or more children as coexecutors or merely by naming a neutral executor.

It is common for a husband or wife to name the survivor as executor. The surviving spouse may be entirely capable of being executor and as such would act with the utmost in economy to the estate. However, a surviving spouse is often at a complete loss when the complex problems of modern business are suddenly thrust upon him or her. Under such circumstances the surviving spouse might welcome the services of a friend or the trust department of a bank or trust company as coexecutor. When a bank or trust company acts as coexecutor, it usually maintains physical custody of bonds, securities, and other properties of the estate, subject, of course, to the right of the coexecutor to inspect the properties and records during business hours.

Other than to pay funeral charges and take necessary measures for preservation of the estate, an executor cannot act until the will is admitted to probate by the court and he is appointed and qualified. There may, however, be certain urgent matters which require attention before the executor can formally qualify. If the deceased was engaged in a going business, it should continue to operate. If there are perishable assets in the estate, they should be protected. It may be necessary to arrange for funds to take care of expenses incidental to the operation of a going business or for the decedent's last illness. In choosing your executor you should consider the willingness and ability of the person or institution named to take immediate action. This includes petitioning the court for appointment as special administrator of the estate with such prescribed powers as are required pending admission of the will to probate and the appointment of the executor.

Telling Your Executor Your Intentions

An executor should be consulted before being named in a will to determine whether he or she is willing to act. The proposed executor may be unwilling or unable to assume the responsibility. You then can ascertain the reason and accommodate the concerns or select someone else. If your will provides for the executor to exercise discretion to resolve conflicts between your beneficiaries, you should discuss your expectations so your executor will have had the benefit of your personal guidance in what could be a difficult situation. Moreover, you may wish to organize all your papers in one location so that your executor does not have to hunt for them and run the risk of mishandling an asset or worse yet missing an asset altogether. Some find a simple accordian file with a separate slot devoted to each asset very helpful. After the will is prepared, it is a good practice to furnish the executor with a copy or to tell him where the original will is located for safekeeping.

Consider the case of John and Mary Doe. They were a married couple with three small children. John and Mary had separate wills that provided if they should die in a common disaster or within a short time of one another, their estates were to be handled by an executor and then a trustee for the benefit of their three children. The contingency happened, but neither John nor Mary had advised the executor of his nomination nor of the location of the wills. Administration proceedings of the estate were initiated under the mistaken belief that the wills did not exist.

Eventually the wills were found, and the executor named offered them for probate and qualified as executor. The administrations taken out before the discovery of the wills were closed, and the properties of the estates were handed over to the qualified executor. Extra time and expense could have been avoided if John and Mary Doe had advised their executor of the location of their wills.

Attributes of an Executor

Considerations in choosing the executor are much the same as those for choosing a business partner. The necessary attributes may be summarized as follows:

- *Integrity.* An executor should have the ultimate interests of the heirs in mind at all times. This requires soundness of moral principal and character. He must be unselfish and honest in the handling of the estate.

- *Business ability.* Sound business judgment, combined with actual experience, is a desired quality. Many economies result from experience, and the testator's ultimate aim is to see that as much of the estate as possible passes to the beneficiaries.
- *Executorship ability.* The handling of an estate requires knowledge of the rights and responsibilities of an executor and the ability to carry them out. With larger estates, knowledge of both income and estate taxation is necessary.
- *Availability.* The time a person has to devote to the handling of the estate depends on its size and complexity. If an executor is to keep the best interests of the beneficiaries in mind, he must have the time to devote to the executorship. In handling large estates, the duties may be so time consuming that an individual executor would have to neglect his personal business interests. In such a case a trust institution should be considered, since it has available officers and employees specially trained in handling estate matters.
- *Impartiality.* Whether the executor is the surviving spouse, child, friend, or a trust institution, complete impartiality must be given to all heirs under the will. Such impartiality may be impossible from a member of the family. If the testator believes this to be the case, he should consider someone outside of the family.
- *Discretion.* Handling an estate may bring an executor into contact with family problems which neither the testator nor his survivors want publicly aired. It is therefore important that the executor be a person who will conduct estate matters confidentially. It is his privilege to serve the deceased, and it is your right to expect matters that were held in confidence during your lifetime to be so maintained after your death.

Summary

You intend for the accumulation of a lifetime to be handled prudently. You should, therefore, select an executor who possesses sound business judgment tempered with concern for your beneficiaries.

In recent years people have given more thought to planning their estates than in the past. This is attributable to the ever growing difficulty of accumulating, managing, and preserving property. Taxation and its adverse effects are of special concern. A will, no matter how simple, should be prepared for every property owner. Preparation of the will should include earnest attention to the selection of an executor. An executor, in order to serve the estate in the best possible way must, like the operator of a successful business, have the necessary experience, knowledge, and seasoned judgment as well as the time to devote to estate affairs.

8
When Is My Estate Valued and Why?

Valuation During Life

An estate is valued during life for one main reason—to obtain facts to plan and carry out the most efficient and economical transfer of the estate to the persons who are to receive it. It may be valued any number of times so the plan may be revised as values and circumstances change.

This is true whether the estate is large or small because the smaller estate can ill afford an expense that planning could have saved.

These valuations are your opportunities to determine whether your estate consists of the desired kinds of property and how far these properties will go in carrying out your intentions, whether they are to protect a spouse, furnish an education for children, or whatever.

With a valuation, you have the opportunity to decide how the estate's transfer will be made and to learn what will be the ultimate costs and consequences of the alternatives for your family. You may choose whether the order of descent and distribution of your estate will be determined by law or by your utilizing the many other choices which are available only if you elect to use them during your life. Only by knowing values and purposes can the most efficient and economical transfer of the properties be planned and achieved.

Every person makes some provision for his property—knowingly or unknowingly—when he or she makes a will, delays making a will, or simply decides not to make a will. It is vital for you to understand how much it will cost your family if you do not plan and how much can be saved by planning. Most people are pleasantly surprised to learn that the cost of planning may be quite small compared to the savings.

Valuation After Death

In general there are two occasions for valuing an estate after the death of the owner. In California, the first occasion usually is pursuant to the California Probate Code which requires valuation of the probate estate and which describes those assets to be valued by the executor or administrator and those to be valued by the probate referee.

This first valuation should also include the nonprobate estate subject to taxation, such as joint tenancy assets and certain types of life insurance. Then it can be determined whether the federal estate tax laws apply. If they do, a second opportunity to value the estate is provided by the federal tax laws.

As pointed out in Chapter 2, the California Probate Code provides procedures to be applied to the probate estate. This code also provides alternative procedures that are available depending on the date-of-death value of certain assets in the estate. We will now discuss these very economical and useful procedures.

Valuation for Special Nonprobate Purposes

The California Probate Code provides for special handling of small estates in three principal situations.

First, a decedent's estate may be collected by the declaration or affidavit of those entitled to succeed to it, when the decedent left no real property nor lien thereon in California and the value of his property in California, excluding amounts due for services in the armed forces of the United States and excluding any other salary from any employment of $5,000 or less (including compensation for unused vacations), does not exceed $30,000. Joint tenancy property, life insurance, retirement benefits and certain other contractual rights that terminate at death, motor vehicles, mobile homes, commercial coaches, as well as community or quasi-community property passing to the surviving spouse, are excluded in determining the $30,000 value. This procedure is available whether the decedent died with or without a will. It is unnecessary to procure letters of administration or await probate of the will.

A spouse, child, grandchild, parent, brother or sister, nephew or niece of the decedent, or conservator or guardian of any of them, who is entitled to succeed to the property, is entitled to collect the personal property, including money due, upon furnishing a declaration showing a right to it to the appropriate persons. This procedure may also be used by the sole beneficiary or by all of the beneficiaries under the will regardless of whether they are related to the decedent.

Second, bank accounts not exceeding the total sum of $500 may be collected by the surviving spouse of a decedent whose estate, irrespective of its character as real or personal property, does not exceed $5,000 in value. A declaration is furnished to the bank by the surviving spouse showing his or her right to the deposit.

Third, if a decedent leaves a surviving spouse or a minor child or children and the net value of the whole estate, exclusive of property held in joint tenancy, over and above all liens and encumbrances at the time of death and any homestead interest set apart to the surviving spouse, does not exceed $20,000, the estate may be set aside to the surviving spouse if there is one, and if not, then to the minor child or children.

Counsel should be consulted regarding the final changes in these valuable procedures effective January 1, 1985.

Inventory Valuation

In the event there is an administration of the estate, either by an executor, an administrator, or a public administrator, the Probate Code specifies that an inventory of the estate must be filed by the personal representative within three months of appointment. An appraisement or valuation is made for each article of property included in the inventory. After appraisal the homestead and exempt property can then be set aside. This inventory and appraisement also indicates to any creditors the extent of the estate for the payment of their claims.

The inventory and appraisement furnishes the basis from which the executor or administrator must account to the beneficiaries for the proper management of the estate, the payment of claims, and the delivery of the proper share to the persons so entitled. The inventory and appraisement must be corrected and supplemented if there are any omissions of properties or if additional properties are discovered. Any interested person, including any beneficiary or creditor, may bring such errors to the attention of the court for correction.

The inventory and appraisement also serves as a basis for the procedure of withdrawing an estate from administration once administration has been granted by the probate court. It further gives a basis for the amount of any bond required of the personal representative during the course of administration as well as providing the foundation for computing the statutory commissions for the executor or administrator and the statutory fees for the attorney.

Valuation for Tax Purposes

Regardless of any appraisement made during the course of proceedings under the Probate Code, there must be a valuation for tax purposes. There is a practical as well as a legal necessity to demonstrate either that no tax is due or that taxes due have been paid. This is done to enable the beneficiaries of the estate to dispose of their shares when they so desire and to give them good title to their properties.

If a federal estate tax return is required to be filed, there is a second occasion to value the estate after death. An election may be made as to whether the tax determination shall be based on the value of the estate at the decedent's death or on the alternative valuation made six months after death.

It has been said that the purpose of this federal election, born of the Depression, is to provide tax relief where there has been a decline in the values of the estate after the decedent's death. While this provision may give such relief, the decision to use it may also be used to advantage when values have increased during the six months. In certain cases a beneficiary may desire the higher estate tax valuation to obtain a higher basis in the property for future depreciation or to minimize income taxes if it is contemplated that a gain will be realized on a future sale of the property. Careful comparison of the estate tax rates with the income tax rates of the individuals will determine whether to use higher or lower estate tax valuations.

The proper use of the election might likewise determine whether any federal estate taxes are due on the estate. If elected, the alternate valuation must then be used for all property, subject to a few special rules. First, if the alternate valuation date is used, any property distributed, sold, exchanged, or otherwise disposed of within the six month period is valued as of the date of such disposition. Secondly, the value of any interest which is affected by a mere lapse of time, such as the paying out of an annuity or the expiration of a patent, is not entitled to be revalued where the revaluation reflects only the effect of the passage of time. We will be discussing the federal estate tax in Chapter 11 and California's new estate tax in Chapter 12.

Summary

Valuation as discussed here, whether for planning, fixing family allowances, determining taxes due, or not due, or using the alternate valuation date, is the determination of the market value of the property on the proper dates. Valuation may be determined by a variety of methods depending on the type of property involved.

It should be noted that the valuation of an estate's assets may be critically important in determining:

1. Whether the estate qualifies for an installment payment of a portion of the federal estate tax at substantially reduced interest rates where a significant part of the estate consists of a farm or a closely held business interest.
2. Whether the estate qualifies for "special use" valuation where a significant portion of the estate consists of a farm or real property used in a trade or business, rather than the standard valuation of property reflecting its "highest and best use."
3. Whether the estate qualifies to redeem stock in a closely held corporation, and avoid the dividend tax, to the extent of death taxes and funeral and administration expenses.

These benefits are discussed in greater detail in Chapter 20. You should plan ahead with professionals to make sure your estate qualifies for the benefits you wish. Proper planning in advance can avoid the needless loss of valuable alternatives at a time when your family can least afford it. By proper valuation and planning during your life, both your desires and the best interests of your beneficiaries can be protected.

9

What Will Probate Cost?

Of universal interest is the question "What will probate cost my estate?" The answer involves careful consideration of the size, type, and location of the present and future assets constituting the estate, any tax complications present, the simplicity or complexity of the disposition of the estate, the extent and type of debts, and various other factors.

This chapter will deal with costs and expenses in relatively routine administrations. It will not cover probate intricacies in unusual situations, complicated probate litigation, or appeals to California appellate courts.

Probate Costs and Bond Premiums—The Well-Drawn Will

A lawyer can make an estimate of probate costs once he knows whether bond has been waived, the nature and extent of the decedent's assets, whether there is a probability of litigation, and similar facts.

If bond is not waived in the will or by all of the beneficiaries, an individual appointed executor or administrator must post bond. If a bond is given by a surety company, the amount must be equal to the value of the personal property plus the value of the probable annual income of all the estate's property. If a bond is given instead by individual persons, the amount must be twice the value of the personal property plus twice the value of the probable annual income of the estate's real property. Surety bond premiums cost about $2.50 to $5.00 per $1,000 depending upon the total amount. The California Probate Code authorizes deposit of estate assets in a California bank or trust company. This may reduce the cost when bond has not been waived. It is important to discuss with counsel the consequences of waiving bond in a will before doing so.

Probate Referee Fees

The probate referee appraises certain property in the decedent's estate. The probate referee's fee is set by the California Probate Code providing for a commission of one tenth of one percent of the total value of the assets he appraises with a minimum fee of $75.00 and a maximum fee of $10,000. However, the court may allow a fee in excess of the maximum if the court determines that the reasonable value of the referee's services exceeds such amount. In addition to the commission, each probate referee is entitled to receive the actual and necessary expenses allowed by the court.

The probate referee appraises those assets of the decedent subject to the probate administration and listed in the estate inventory that the executor or administrator is not required to appraise himself. The referee if requested may also appraise the property passing outside of probate in joint tenancy or in a trust for estate tax purposes or for establishing evidence of basis at death.

Most of the probate referee's time is spent on appraising the decedent's real property and business interests and conferring with the executor or administrator and his attorney informally about the decedent's property. All of this takes considerable time and expertise.

Executor's or Administrator's Commission Set by Law

As is the case in practically every state, the commission (fee) of the executor or the administrator is set by law and is usually referred to as "statutory commissions." Additional compensation may be allowed for extraordinary services. Under the California Probate Code, an executor or administrator is allowed, out of the estate, necessary expenses in the care, management, and settlement of the estate. For his services, he is allowed statutory commissions "upon the amount of estate accounted for by him" as follows: for the first $15,000 at the rate of 4%, for the next $85,000 at the rate of 3%, for the next $900,000 at the rate of 2% and for all above $1,000,000 at the rate of 1%.

Although the will may provide for other compensation, the executor may renounce those provisions and claim statutory compensation. Additionally, the probate court may allow the executor or administrator additional compensation for extraordinary services such as sales or mortgages of real or personal property, contested or litigated claims against the estate, the preparation of estate, income, or other tax returns, the adjustment or litigation of any of these taxes, the carrying on of the decedent's business pursuant to an order of the court, and other litigation or special services as may have been necessary.

The probate court makes all orders for allowance of statutory and extra compensation. The executor or administrator may apply to the probate court for partial allowance of his commissions anytime after four months from the issuance of letters testamentary or of administration. Usually, if statutory commissions adequately compensate for the services of the executor or administrator, the probate court will grant no further allowance for what might well be considered to be extraordinary services. Probate judges are alert to this problem and deal fairly with both the estate and the personal representative.

Attorney Fees Set by Law

California is one of a minority of states with statutes that fix the rates of attorney fees in probate. California's rates are among the lowest. In fact, the fees are lower than those in most all other states, regardless of how they are fixed. Fee schedules protect the public and the attorneys. Without schedules, fee setting could become chaotic and planning more difficult.

Attorney fees for conducting the ordinary probate proceedings are the same as the commissions to executors and administrators. The probate court may allow attorneys such further amounts as the court deems just and reasonable for extraordinary services. The court determines whether the claimed services are extraordinary and sets the fee for them. An attorney may ask the court for partial payment on the fee after four months from the issuance of letters.

As we discussed, the commissions of the executor or administrator and attorney are based "upon the amount of estate accounted for." That phrase has reference to the inventory and appraisement of the decedent's property subject to administration in the probate court. There is a popular misunderstanding regarding the items of property that belonged to a decedent which are considered in fixing the commissions of an executor or administrator and the fees of his attorney. Generally speaking, the commissions and fees are calculated by multiplying the statutory rates by the total value reported in the inventory and appraisement of the probate estate plus gains over appraisal value on sales, plus receipts, less losses on sales, without subtracting encumbrances on property in the estate. For example, a $100,000 house with a $60,000 trust deed on it is valued at $100,000 since encumbrances are not subtracted. However, not every item of property belonging to a decedent is included in the inventory and thus is not considered in the computation of commissions and fees. As we discussed in Chapter 1, the probate estate does not include joint tenancy property, insurance not payable to the estate, property in trust not payable to the estate, annuities, pensions, social security payments, and in most cases, community property passing to a surviving spouse.

To estimate commissions and fees, let us look at Table 9-1. If the probate estate is valued at $15,000, we add to the executor's commissions of $600 the attorney fee of $600 for a total of $1,200. Similarly for a $100,000 probate estate, the total of the commissions and fees is $6,300. This does not include payment for the extraordinary services described above. Chapter 10 discusses how to save these commissions and fees in the appropriate case with a simple probate avoidance living trust. The following section addresses another type of trust—those established during probate proceedings.

Table 9-1
California Statutory Fees and Commissions
(Prob C §§901, 910)

Amount accounted for in probate estate*	Executor's commission (same as attorney fees)	+	% on next $
0–15,000	4% of estate		
$ 15,000	$ 600		3%
50,000	1,650		
100,000	3,150		2%
150,000	4,150		
200,000	5,150		
300,000	7,150		
400,000	9,150		
500,000	11,150		
600,000	13,150		
700,000	15,150		
800,000	17,150		
900,000	19,150		
1,000,000	21,150		1%
1,250,000	23,650		
1,500,000	26,150		
2,000,000	31,150		
3,000,000	41,150		
4,000,000	51,150		

Additional amounts are subject to the 1% rate.

* The estate accounted for includes the inventory, income during administration, and capital gains on sales over inventory value, less capital losses on sales under inventory value.

Source: Regents of the University of California, California Continuing Education of the Bar.

Administration of Testamentary Trusts

Where a trust is created under a will, called a testamentary trust, the trustee takes over the trust administration when assets of the estate are delivered to the trustee by the executor pursuant to the probate court's order or decree of distribution. Such distribution may occur through an order of preliminary distribution of the estate or at the time of its final distribution. In connection with such trusts, a trustee or beneficiary may petition the court with respect to many matters specified by law. During the course of administration of the trust, the trustee furnishes annual accountings to show how he has administered the trust. In some cases, he may file accountings with the court in order to have the accounts settled, the investments approved and the fees confirmed. Under some circumstances these trusts may be removed from court supervision.

Trustees' Fees

Bank and trust company fees for acting as a trustee vary widely. They seldom consent to serve as a trustee under a will for a flat fee. Probate courts in California are not uniform in their fixing, directing, or allowing payment of trustees' fees, nor are banks or trust companies uniform in their requests for fees. In any event, the will must now state that any trust created by the will is subject to the continuing jurisdiction of the superior court if the trustee is to be required to seek court approval of the fees. Generally California courts allow fees to trustees equal to between 10% and 20% of the trust's annual income. The smaller the trust the larger the percentage, for banks do insist upon a minimum fee. A trust with an exceptionally large annual income may pay as little as 5% of that income for the trustee's annual services.

You should have a full and frank discussion with a proposed trustee regarding all your expectations before the final selection. Whether the trustee is to be an individual or an institution should be carefully considered. The value of communication with the trustee prior to making the selection cannot be emphasized enough.

Fees of Attorneys for Trustees

The trustee calls upon the attorney for any and all legal advice and services affecting the trust estate. The attorney is not free to take employment in conflict with the trust. The probate court may confirm the fee for the attorney at the same time it confirms the trustee's fee if the will expressly requires continuing superior court jurisdiction over the trust. There is no uniformity among attorneys or courts regarding either the amount of the fee for the attorney or the manner in which it is fixed. It may range from one tenth or less of the trustee's fee to an amount equal to or even exceeding the trustee's fee.

What About the Cost of a Will?

You should not hesitate to inquire about the legal expense. It should be discussed frankly so that reasonable arrangements can be made in advance of the preparation of the will. The fee for estate planning and for drafting wills and trusts is based in large part upon the time actually spent in such services rather than upon the value of the estate.

Drafting a will providing for a trust or drafting a living (inter vivos) trust can be one of the most difficult tasks undertaken by a lawyer. The complexity of present tax laws alone makes it necessary for the lawyer to spend substantially more time keeping up with tax law changes and decisions than in bygone days. Nevertheless, a properly drafted will or trust remains one of the greatest values available today.

Summary

California has one of the finest probate administrative systems in America. With a proper will, probate costs are at a minimum, and there is no bonding expense. The fees of executors and administrators can be estimated once the gross value and nature of the estate and probable income and disbursements are known.

In California, attorney fees for services to the executor or administrator are set by law. When a testator does not make a proper will, the cost of administering his estate most likely will be higher than if a properly prepared will had been made by an attorney who was familiar with expense-cutting provisions, meanings of legal terms, consequences of legal principles, requirements for executing wills, and the necessity for definiteness.

A person needing the services of an attorney should not hesitate to discuss the fee. Substantial savings in probate expenses and taxes can result from proper planning, which, to the pleasant surprise of most, is accomplished at a small cost in comparison to the amount saved. Of all the alternatives available today, by far the most costly may be to do nothing at all.

10
The Revocable Living Trust

The revocable trust is an instrument in estate planning that has gained widespread popularity. The general concept is easy to understand. An owner (*grantor*) transfers property to a trustee to be managed for the benefit of a beneficiary.

In the simple probate avoidance trust, the owner (grantor) transfers property to himself as trustee to be managed for himself as a beneficiary. He can always change the assets in the trust. He can also change the terms and beneficiaries of the trust if he wishes.

There are two broad categories of trusts—the living trust and the testamentary trust. A *living trust* is created during the grantor's lifetime with a trust instrument, and a *testamentary trust* is created upon the grantor's death in his will.

There are two classes of living trusts, revocable and irrevocable. A *revocable trust,* as its name implies, is one that can be cancelled or changed during its existence. An *irrevocable trust* is one which cannot be altered. In Chapter 13 we will examine some of the most valuable irrevocable trusts.

In the typical revocable living trust a grantor transfers property to himself or another as trustee under a written agreement. The agreement provides for the trustee to pay the grantor all of the income from the trust during his lifetime, together with such amounts of principal as may be requested. It also provides that the grantor can amend or revoke the trust or change the trustee at any time.

The revocable living trust typically allows the grantor to change the assets in the trust whenever he wishes. The grantor as trustee can buy new assets, sell or give away old assets, and even receive new assets into the trust as gifts from others.

Typically, the grantor appoints himself trustee during his lifetime and then names his spouse, adult child, bank, or advisor as trustee on his death. Upon the death of the grantor, the trust becomes irrevocable. With a fully funded living trust (one to which all the grantor's assets have been transferred), probate is avoided. The provisions of the trust agreement which apply to the administration and distribution of the trust assets after the death of the grantor become operative and are carried out immediately. There is no delay nor publicity normally necessary to the probate of a will.

A revocable living trust has a number of advantages when compared with a testamentary trust; however, the benefits and cost of probating some or all of the assets must be weighed in each case. Where probate is not advantageous, the costs may be saved and the delays avoided with a fully funded revocable living trust.

Advantages of the Revocable Trust

Management Uninterrupted by Incapacity

If a large part or all of your assets are placed in the trust during your lifetime, the revocable trust can afford continuous management of the trust assets regardless of your physical or mental incapacity. If you are the initial trustee, your successor trustee named in the trust may assume your duties as trustee upon your incapacity, without the costs and publicity of a conservatorship proceeding if the trust so provides. When you are restored to competence, you can resume your duties as your own trustee if you wish.

If you name another individual or a bank as trustee, then your later becoming incompetent does not affect the trustee's power to continue to protect and manage the assets.

Where you have named another as trustee and you desire to retain investment control of the trust assets, the trust agreement can provide that, while you are alive and remain competent, no purchases or sales of the trust assets or any other important actions can be made without your approval. Should you become unable to manage your assets, either through mental or physical disabilities, the revocable trust is the ideal instrument for continuing proper management.

In contrast to the durable power of attorney that we will discuss in Chapter 17, a nondurable power of attorney given to another person to manage the grantor's affairs will be automatically revoked upon the grantor's mental incapacity. Proceedings for the appointment of a conservator for a person upon his becoming senile or incompetent or upon his drifting in and out of lucid mental periods can provoke unpleasant family quarrels. It certainly will involve court control of the assets of the incompetent, large legal and accounting fees, bonding fees, severe restrictions on investments, and much red tape.

The revocable living trust is an excellent answer to these problems. The trustee can perform all the necessary management of the trust assets, including the collection of income, the purchase and sale of trust assets, and the management of a closely held business or real estate. In addition the trustee can make payment of hospital, nursing and doctor bills, and other expenses of the grantor. When the period of temporary crisis ends, the trust can always be revoked by the grantor if he so desires, or the grantor may again take up active participation in his trust and either leave the assets with the trustee or become trustee himself. If the grantor dies, the trust acts like the grantor's will insofar as the assets in the trust are concerned.

Management for the Estate Owner

A revocable trust is a valuable aid to the busy estate owner who does not have time to study the stock market or to do the many other things that are involved in managing the investment of valuable trust assets. A professional trustee can supply experienced investment guidance and free a busy executive or professional person from the worries that might interfere with the pursuit of his business or profession, while at the same time assuring him of continuous expert investment management of his trust assets and avoidance of probate.

Segregation of Assets

A revocable trust also has the advantage of preventing certain properties from becoming commingled with other property. For example, if a wife has inherited property from her parents and she desires that the property be kept separate from the community property she and her husband own, she can place her inherited separate property within a revocable trust. The trustee can maintain adequate records to keep that property segregated from the community assets. Alternatively, her parents could have left the property to her as trustee of her own trust.

Trial Run for a Trustee Other Than Yourself

The revocable trust allows you to observe the operation of the person or bank you would like to manage your estate upon your death. You can then satisfy yourself as to the manner in which your assets will be managed and administered after your death. This will also allow your spouse to become familiar with the trustee and the lawyer, so that old friends, instead of strangers, will be there to take care of your spouse at your death.

Privacy of Disposition of Assets at Death

Another advantage of the revocable trust is the privacy afforded the grantor for the disposition of his estate at his death. Assets placed in a revocable living trust do not become a matter of public court record as is the case with a probated will. Newspaper publicity about the grantor's assets, his beneficiaries, and his disposition plans are thus avoided.

Reduction of Probate Expense

A funded revocable living trust will result in the reduction of probate expenses. The executor's commissions, attorney fees, accounting fees, probate referee fees, and other charges arising from the administration of a deceased person's estate are based to a certain extent on the value of the assets passing under the decedent's will. Keeping property out of the probate estate of the grantor can reduce such charges. If all of a grantor's assets are in a revocable trust at the time of his death, it may not be necessary to go through probate at all. However, this savings may be offset to some degree by the cost of a professional trustee's administering the trust assets during the grantor's lifetime. Where the grantor or the grantor's spouse acts as his own trustee, these costs too can be avoided.

Advantages Over Joint Tenancy

Joint tenancy may prove ill advised generally for California spouses for their community property for three principal reasons:

1. Appreciated property receives a step-up in federal tax basis equal to the date-of-death valuation only as to one half of the property held in joint tenancy as contrasted to a 100% step-up for community property held as community property in trust.
2. Virtually no controls may be applied to the use and disposition of the property in the hands of the surviving joint tenant, compared to the broad controls available for the decedent's half of community property held in trust.
3. Joint tenancy may expose an estate to estate taxes upon the death of the surviving spouse that could easily have been avoided with a bypass trust. See Chapter 13.

The step-up in tax basis available to community property in trust rather than to joint tenancy property could significantly reduce, if not totally eliminate, the federal income tax otherwise imposed on the sale of appreciated property received from a deceased spouse.

Unlike joint tenancy, a trust will insure that property left to a surviving spouse will be protected from ill-intended individuals as well as the temptations of the marketplace. The spouse who is concerned about protecting his or her property for the children and avoiding disposition of the property by her husband's next wife, or vice versa, may avoid this danger of joint tenancy by putting her half of the community and all of her separate property in a living trust that becomes irrevocable on death.

Avoidance of Will Contest

A revocable trust is less vulnerable to attack by disgruntled heirs than a will. It is rather easy for a relative who is an heir to contest the probate of a will even for specious reasons. It is quite expensive and time consuming for the executor to successfully resist a contest. Accordingly, a settlement just to avoid litigation may be economically required even though contrary to the testator's intentions.

A challenge to the validity of a revocable living trust may be made on the same grounds as a contest to a will (lack of capacity or undue influence). However, it is generally more difficult to establish such defects when the trust has operated for years. The litigation does not tie up the trust assets in the same manner as a will contest ties up the probate assets. Since little in a will has any effect or substance until after the will has been admitted to probate by formal court order, the assets may be tied up until the will contest is settled. By contrast a living trust remains in full force and effect at the death of the grantor, and if there is a contest to the trust, the trustee has the assets in his hands generally with authority to use them to defend the trust.

Uninterrupted Management at Death

A revocable trust provides a means for avoiding any interruption in the management of the trust's assets upon the death of the grantor. Stocks, securities, real estate, and so on can continue to be managed, and debts, expenses of last illness, funeral bills, taxes, and so on can be promptly paid. Further, there is no delay incurred in providing for the grantor's family immediately after his death. This is important when the trust property consists of assets which require timely attention and the family has on-going financial requirements.

Avoidance of Probate in Other States

If the grantor owns property physically located in different states, it may be possible to avoid expensive and time-consuming probate proceedings in those states by conveying the property to a trustee during the grantor's lifetime. However, if real estate in other states is to be placed in a revocable trust, it is important to make sure that the laws of the state where the property is located allow a trustee from another state to act within that state, will not create property tax problems, and are not otherwise inconsistent with the provisions of the trust.

Tax Treatment of the Revocable Trust

Assets in a revocable living trust continue to be taxed to the grantor as if owned by him personally. Income is reported directly on the grantor's individual tax return. No gift tax is due when a grantor creates a revocable trust. In California, transfer of real estate to a revocable trust will not affect property taxes. Upon the grantor's death, all of the property in the trust is included in his gross estate for estate tax purposes.

The assets in the revocable trust acquire an income tax basis equal to their fair market value at the grantor's death, and both the husband's and wife's half of the community property held in a properly drafted trust will also acquire a new federal income tax basis on the death of either spouse. Upon the grantor's death, the trust becomes irrevocable, and the same tax advantages available to a testamentary trust are available to the living trust. These include reduction and in some cases elimination of estate tax on the surviving spouse's death and the creation of several different tax entities for federal income tax purposes. See the discussion of sprinkling trusts in Chapter 13.

Availability of Subchapter "S" Election

If stock in a closely held corporation which has elected Subchapter "S" for federal income tax purposes is placed in a trust, the corporation can continue in such capacity as long as the trust is revocable.

Limitation on Amount of Discounted Treasury Bonds Accepted at Par for Estate Tax Payment

As will be discussed in the next chapter, certain U.S. Treasury bonds which were purchased at a discount can be redeemed at par plus accrued interest at the death of the owner for the purpose of having the proceeds applied to the payment of federal estate taxes. Such bonds held by a revocable living trust are redeemable only in the amount which the trustee of the trust is required to pay under the terms of the trust instrument for the federal estate tax. Therefore, it may be desirable to keep the ownership of such bonds in the name of the owner himself, rather than to place them in a revocable trust, unless a special provision is included in the trust that requires the trustee to pay the estate tax at least in an amount not less than the par value plus accrued interest of the bonds.

Application of the "Throwback Rule"

An estate may accumulate income during the period of administration without involving the throwback rule. This income tax rule taxes some of the income to the beneficiaries of a trust upon later distribution of assets to them. The relative income tax advantages enjoyed by the probate estate should be examined in each case. They may be obtained by planning to probate selected assets where the taxes saved exceed the costs incurred.

Community Property and Revocable Trusts

If community property is to be placed in a revocable trust, both spouses should join in the execution of the trust agreement and any amendment. The provisions of the trust must be drafted with special care to preserve the character of community property.

Summary

In the appropriate case, a fully funded living trust can avoid the significant costs and delays of probate and save considerable time and money for the family. By using a revocable living trust, you may select a trustee to manage your assets in the event you should become incapacitated, rather than having a person appointed by the court do so. While competent, you can continue to manage your assets as your own trustee, or you may turn some or all management over to an independent trustee. The creation of the trust during your lifetime also allows you to study the management of your assets by an independent trustee to be sure the trustee will handle them in the proper manner after your death. The management of the property placed in a revocable living trust continues uninterrupted at death. Such continuity may be particularly important when the property managed is a closely held business needing constant attention. By placing property owned in other states in a revocable living trust, probate within those states may be avoided.

To completely avoid probate you must transfer each of your assets to the revocable living trust while you are alive. You have the choice of planning to probate any, all, or none of your assets. The judicious and selective use of the benefits of probate should be discussed with counsel. Probate offers procedures for protection against creditors (particularly tort claimants), resolving disputes among beneficiaries, selling real estate in an "auction atmosphere," which may or may not generate a higher price, as well as saving income taxes, and providing other benefits.

There is no general rule that applies to everyone. The benefits and costs must be weighed in each individual case so that avoidable costs are not incurred and substantial benefits are not sacrificed.

11
Federal Estate Taxes

The federal estate tax system did not come into being until 1916. Proper planning can eliminate this tax in many estates.

When the law was first enacted, the tax was to minimize the transfer of great family wealth from generation to generation. This concept was not new; English common law had variations of the death tax for centuries.

But the scope of the federal estate tax extended beyond anyone's expectations. Reform in 1976 attempted to eliminate the tax on small and modest estates, but inflation eroded the value of these changes. The Reagan Administration proposed a major overhaul of our tax system in 1981, and the estate tax rules were included.

This chapter will first highlight the key estate tax changes brought by the Economic Recovery Tax Act of 1981 (E.R.T.A.) and then describe how the tax is now computed. Finally, we will raise and answer some of the most frequently asked questions about the tax and its minimization.

What Changes Did E.R.T.A. Make in the Estate Tax?

1. *The amount of property that each person can own without paying taxes has been increased.* The amount of property exempt from tax in 1984 is $325,000. This exemption actually results from a tax credit of $96,300. To the extent the credit is used for taxable gifts during life, it is not available at death. The credit and its exemption equivalent are presently scheduled to increase until 1987, but beware of the effects of inflation on your estate when reading the following table.

For Decedents Dying In the Year	Equivalent Amount Exempt from Tax	Tax Credit
1983	$275,000	$ 79,300
1984	$325,000	$ 96,300
1985	$400,000	$121,800
1986	$500,000	$155,800
1987 and thereafter	$600,000	$192,800

2. *The amount of property that one spouse may give to another spouse without any tax is now unlimited.* The tax law has never been quite certain how to treat transfers between husband and wife. Community property states had one set of rules, and separate property states had another. The federal system tried to reconcile the two different property laws but usually with mixed results.

   In addition, it was argued, the spouses were really a single economic unit and should be treated as such. The joint income tax return recognized this reality.

   Finally, the financial burden imposed on a surviving spouse by reason of the tax on the estate of the decedent spouse placed the family in a precarious, and oftentimes, calamitous position.

   The federal law now provides an unlimited deduction on qualifying gifts by one spouse to the other whether the gift is made during life or at death. The absence of a tax on this transfer, however, does not mean that no tax will ever be due. When the surviving spouse ultimately dies, a tax on the estate in excess of the exemption amount for that spouse will still be payable. In fact, adding the first spouse's assets on top of the second spouse's may result in a higher tax than if the tax were paid separately on each.

   This unfortunate result can be minimized with proper planning which will be discussed later in this chapter.

3. *The rate at which certain estates are taxed will be lower.* Large estates (in excess of $5,000,000) were formerly subject to a tax rate of 70%. When combined with state inheritance taxes, the total tax burden could exceed 85% of the estate.

   Rates are gradually being reduced for the larger estates. By 1985, the maximum rate for any estate will be 50% on amounts in excess of $2,500,000.

Additional significant changes were also made dealing with the long term financing of estate taxes, special valuations of real property used in farms and closely held businesses, special redemptions of stock, and others. (See Chapter 20.)

How Is the Federal Estate Tax Computed?

The basic principle of federal estate taxation is the notion that the government is entitled to a tax upon the transfer of wealth from one person to another. A transfer may be made during lifetime (in which case a gift tax may be imposed) or upon death (at which time a death tax may be imposed).

As with most simple rules, the exceptions, conditions, and variations make applying the death tax extremely complex. The tax is only paid if the transfer when added to the accumulation of prior transfers exceeds the exemption level we discussed earlier. The tax is computed on the net fair market value of the asset conveyed, after all debts, liens, and encumbrances are subtracted.

The formula for determining the estate tax is, simply described,

1. Value the decedent's "gross estate"
   Subtract: Deductions allowable by law
   Add: Taxable gifts made after December 31, 1976, not included in the gross estate
   To Obtain: Tax base
2. Compute the tentative tax on the tax base using the unified rate schedule.
3. Subtract the gift tax on post-1976 gifts applying the rates in effect on decedent's death.
4. Subtract available tax credits.
5. Result is the estate tax payable.

To understand this formula, we should understand some key considerations.

What Is the Gross Estate?

The federal estate tax is imposed upon the transfer of a decedent's property or gross estate to his beneficiaries.

In a community property state, the decedent's gross estate includes the entire value of all his separate property as well as his half interest in all community property. The tax is based on the estate's fair market value on the decedent's death, or at the option of the taxpayer, six months from the date of death (or as of the dates of sale, distribution, or other disposition during this six month period). The gross estate includes insurance on the decedent's life in which he possessed any "incident of ownership" in the policy. An incident of ownership includes the right to change the beneficiary, the right to borrow against the policy, or other similar rights available under the insurance policy.

The value of the gross estate for tax purposes includes many things besides property owned outright by the decedent, such as real property, stocks, bonds, cash, and personal effects, at the time of his death. The property owner should be aware that the following items may be included in the value of the gross estate:

1. Property transferred by the owner during his life in which he retained certain rights. These rights include the right to use the property for life, to revoke the transfer, or to designate the one who should possess or enjoy the property. Where the transfer does not take effect until after the owner's death, the property transferred is also included in the gross estate.
2. Interests in property owned by him and others as joint tenants with right of survivorship.
3. Certain property in which the owner held the right to direct the disposition of the property or appoint it to others.

Under the law that existed before E.R.T.A., gifts made within three years of death were presumed to be made "in contemplation of death" in the hopes of avoiding death taxes. These gifts were brought back into the owner's gross estate as if the donor had never made the transfer. This rule is, for the most part, no longer applicable. Such transfers will not be brought back into the gross estate, although they may be subject to gift taxes at the time of the original transfer. The exception to this new provision is life insurance.

What Can Be Deducted from the Gross Estate?

Funeral expenses, administration expenses (such as accountant fees, attorney fees, costs of property management, and so on), claims and debts may all be deducted from the gross estate. In community property states the decedent's estate may deduct only one half of the community debts and obligations.

In addition, an unlimited deduction is allowed for gifts made either outright to a surviving spouse or in another qualifying form like the marital deduction trust. Since the day of reckoning will ultimately come when the surviving spouse dies, it is important for the family to make sure that the tax exempt amount ($325,000 in 1984 increasing to $600,000 in 1987) from the estate of the first spouse to die passes tax free on the death of the surviving spouse. This is accomplished with the bypass trust described in Chapter 13.

The excess over the tax exempt amount may be placed in a marital deduction trust. This will eliminate the estate tax on the death of the first spouse altogether. A marital deduction trust that most suits an individual's intent may be selected. Both the surviving spouse and the children may be protected. (See Chapter 13.)

There is also a new technique that will qualify for the unlimited marital deduction and still control both the use and disposition of the property. Congress felt that the enjoyment of a decedent's property by the surviving spouse should not prevent the decedent from deciding who gets the property when the surviving spouse dies. The decedent establishes a trust with the property passing to certain individuals on the surviving spouse's death. The surviving spouse receives all the income from the trust for his or her life. The decedent's executor must elect to defer paying the tax on the trust until the surviving spouse dies.

This technique combines tax deferral with dispositive control. It may be of interest to spouses concerned with preserving the principal of their estate for their children while protecting their surviving spouse with the income. Note, however, that combining both spouse's estates at the survivor's death may actually result in more tax being paid than if some tax were paid on each estate separately.

Qualified gifts to charity may be deducted from the gross estate. Combining the marital and charitable deductions makes the estate tax purely voluntary for those who properly plan. The charitable lead trust should be discussed with counsel. An introduction appears in Chapter 14.

What Are the Tax Rates on a Decedent's Estate?

The tax rate depends upon the size of the estate. The rate begins at 18% for estates up to $10,000 and progresses to 55% (reducing to 50% by 1985) on estates over $3,000,000 (reducing to $2,500,000 by 1985). You should consult your attorney on the status of proposals to delay the reduction to 50% beyond 1985. A full chart of the rates is set out in Table 11-1.

Table 11-1
Federal Estate and Gift Tax Rates
For Decedents Dying after December 31, 1982

A	B	C	D
Amount Subject to Tax			
More Than	But Not More Than	Tax on Amount in Column A	Tax Rate on Excess Over Amount in Column A
$ 0	$ 10,000	$ 0	18%
10,000	20,000	1,800	20
20,000	40,000	3,800	22
40,000	60,000	8,200	24
60,000	80,000	13,000	26
80,000	100,000	18,200	28
100,000	150,000	23,800	30
150,000	250,000	38,800	32
250,000	500,000	70,800	34
500,000	750,000	155,800	37
750,000	1,000,000	248,300	39
1,000,000	1,250,000	345,800	41
1,250,000	1,500,000	448,300	43
1,500,000	2,000,000	555,800	45
2,000,000	2,500,000	780,800	49
2,500,000	3,000,000	1,025,800	53*
3,000,000	—	1,290,800	55*

* The estate and gift tax rate in 1983 between $3,000,000 and $3,500,000 was 57% and above $3,500,000 was 60%, and after 1984 this maximum rate will drop to 50% above $2,500,000.

What Are the Available Tax Credits?

In determining the net tax payable by a decedent's estate several credits are allowed. A credit is a direct reduction of the estate tax (as distinguished from a deduction). We will discuss each credit separately.

Unified credit. As we discussed earlier, the law permits every taxpayer to own an amount of property exempt from estate tax. This exemption was translated from the credit on the tax on property up to the exemption level. For example, a decedent dying in 1985 may own $400,000 of property before any tax is due. This exemption level equates to a unified tax credit of $121,800. If this decedent owned property less than $400,000, the tax otherwise due would be less than the unified credit against the tax. On the other hand, if the estate surpassed $400,000 in 1985, then the tax would be greater than the unified credit, and the excess would be payable.

Credit for state death taxes. A credit is allowed for the amount of any estate, inheritance, or similar tax paid to any state or the District of Columbia with respect to property included in the gross estate. The amount of this credit is subject to various limitations and may be far less than the actual inheritance tax paid to the state. A chart setting forth this tax credit appears as Table 11-2.

California recently repealed its inheritance tax and replaced it with an estate tax exactly equal to the amount of this credit for state death taxes. We will discuss the new California estate tax in Chapter 12.

Credit for pre-1977 gift taxes. A credit is allowed for the gift tax paid on pre-1977 gifts included in the gross estate.

Credit for prior estate taxes paid. A credit is allowed for estate tax previously paid on property inherited from another who died two years after or within a period of up to ten years before the present decedent's death. The maximum credit is allowed if the other decedent died within two years of the present decedent's death; after that, the credit is reduced by 20% every two years. In the third and fourth years, therefore, only 80% of the maximum credit is allowed, and this reduces to 20% in the ninth and tenth year. There is no credit after ten years.

Credit for foreign death taxes. A credit is allowed against the estate tax for any estate, inheritance, or similar tax actually paid to a foreign country by the decedent's estate. This credit is limited by the federal estate tax attributable to such property.

Table 11-2
Maximum Credit against Federal Estate Tax for State Death Taxes

A	B	C	D
Adjusted Taxable Estate (Taxable Estate Minus $60,000) More Than	But Not More Than	Credit on Amount in Column A	Tax Rate on Excess Over Amount in Column A
$ 40,000	$ 90,000	$ 0	0.8%
90,000	140,000	400	1.6
140,000	240,000	1,200	2.4
240,000	440,000	3,600	3.2
440,000	640,000	10,000	4.0
640,000	840,000	18,000	4.8
840,000	1,040,000	27,600	5.6
1,040,000	1,540,000	38,800	6.4
1,540,000	2,040,000	70,800	7.2
2,040,000	2,540,000	106,800	8.0
2,540,000	3,040,000	146,800	8.8
3,040,000	3,540,000	190,800	9.6
3,540,000	4,040,000	238,800	10.4
4,040,000	5,040,000	290,800	11.2
5,040,000	6,040,000	402,800	12.0
6,040,000	7,040,000	522,800	12.8
7,040,000	8,040,000	650,800	13.6
8,040,000	9,040,000	786,800	14.4
9,040,000	10,040,000	930,800	15.2
10,040,000	—	1,082,800	16.0

Payment of the Federal Estate Tax

When Must I Pay the Tax?

The general rule is that any tax due must be paid in cash within nine months of the individual's death. By now, however, you know that exceptions exist to most every rule in law. The burden of paying the tax within this time can be extremely difficult, so understanding the exceptions is important.

What If I Need More Time to Pay?

The IRS has discretion to allow an extension of time for paying the tax up to ten years upon a showing of "reasonable cause" by the executor. Interest, of course, is charged on the unpaid tax. The fact that assets in the estate have to be liquidated, even at a loss, is not normally "reasonable cause." Nor is the cost of borrowing money considered sufficient.

Since few guidelines exist in this area, little reliance should be placed on it for planning purposes.

Can I Pay the Tax in Installments?

Under some circumstances a decedent's estate may qualify for a long term payout of a portion of the death tax and, possibly, favorable financial terms.

The tax attributable to a business interest or a farm may be deferred for up to five years after the tax is due and can then be paid in as many as ten equal annual installments. Keep in mind that only the portion of the tax related to the business interest can be paid with these installments. See our discussion of this benefit in Chapter 20.

Must I Always Pay in Cash?

Not all tax must be paid in cash. If the decedent owned certain issues of U.S. Treasury bonds, known as "flower bonds," they may be redeemed prior to maturity at full par value plus accrued interest in payment of death taxes.

These bonds were issued prior to March 3, 1971, but are still available. The purchase price of the bonds, which typically pay 3% to 4% interest, may be as little as 60% or 70% of par value. Thus buying a flower bond shortly before death is an attractive way to pay tax at a discount. For example, a bond could be purchased by an individual at $6,500 and redeemed by his estate shortly thereafter at $10,000 in payment of the tax.

The key requirement to remember is that the bond must be owned by the decedent prior to death.

Minimizing or Eliminating the Tax

The estate tax has been called a voluntary tax. It is paid in full by those who do not plan. Proper planning can eliminate the tax altogether in some estates and defer or minimize it in others. The various vehicles for keeping this tax money in the family should be thoroughly discussed with counsel. These include the bypass trust, the marital deduction trust, and the charitable lead trust just to name a few.

A pitfall to watch out for with the new unlimited marital deduction is failing to avoid tax on *your* tax exempt amount in the estate of your surviving spouse. Placing this amount in a maximum benefit bypass trust avoids this tax on the death of the surviving spouse while providing the spouse with money to maintain the standard of living you both enjoyed together. This trust may continue for the benefit of your children following your spouse's death. (See Chapter 13.)

Summary

Everyone is given the opportunity by the federal government to plan his estate in such a way as to minimize the effect of the tax. The federal government approves, indeed encourages, proper tax planning and rewards those who act to minimize the tax with substantial savings. We all face income tax annually, but estate taxes are faced by our family after death—a time everyone tends to regard as too remote for present consideration. In an age when building an estate is difficult, each person should familiarize himself with the federal estate tax and prepare for it.

12
California Estate Tax

In 1905, the California legislature enacted an inheritance tax statute forming the basic pattern for California inheritance tax legislation to 1982. In 1982, California's inheritance tax was repealed and replaced by the new California estate tax.

This new tax ("pick-up tax") is applicable only to estates that owe some federal estate tax. It is designed to take advantage of the credit for state death taxes we discussed in the last chapter that allows a certain portion of any death tax paid to a state to count as a credit against the federal estate tax. The California estate tax does not cost the estate any additional taxes. If California had no such tax, there would be no credit against the federal estate tax so what would have been a credit must then be paid to the federal government. The California estate tax merely picks up the amount allowed as a credit against the federal tax. This is why the tax is often called a "pick-up tax."

California will claim the maximum credit allowable if the decedent's estate is entirely within this state's jurisdiction. A proportionate share of the credit will be claimed if the decedent dies owning property subject to the jurisdiction of more than one state.

The administration of the California estate tax is under the direction of the State Controller whose office is in Sacramento. The Controller has broad powers to insure proper enforcement of the tax and may exchange information with the Internal Revenue Service.

A California estate tax return must be filed if a federal tax return is required. The California return must be filed within nine months of the date of death. If the return is not timely filed, there is a penalty equal to 5% of the tax due per month up to a maximum of 25%. However, if an extension to file the federal estate tax return is granted by the Internal Revenue Service, a similar extension will be given for the California return. No penalty is charged during the extension period.

In addition to the penalty for late filing, if the tax is not paid within 9 months of the date of death, it will bear an annual interest of 12% until paid.

13
The Irrevocable Trust

As distinguished from the revocable trust discussed in Chapter 10, the irrevocable trust cannot be revoked or altered by the "grantor," the person who establishes it. The grantor of the trust has given up the right to change his mind and has relinquished the trust property either permanently or for some specific period of time. An irrevocable trust may be created by will or during the lifetime of the grantor by an instrument. It may also result from a revocable trust, which by its terms may become irrevocable upon the death of the grantor.

Why Trusts?

Since the irrevocable trust by definition involves a more permanent form of arrangement than the revocable trust, it seems wise to consider at least briefly some basic background information concerning trusts. A trust is simply a device in which the legal title to property and the right to control it are separated from the right to receive the benefits from it. Historically, the need for such a separation arose from the plight of the person with property who wanted to make provision for his family or friends but feared giving property directly to them because of their inexperience in financial management, their youth, or their irresponsibility. He solved this problem by placing the legal title and management of the property in the hands of a responsible third party. He then stipulated the manner in which the benefits were to be paid to his beneficiaries. The assurance of proper financial management is probably the most important reason for the existence of trusts.

Who Should Be Trustee?

Who should be selected as the trustee to exercise this management? This decision is much more important in an irrevocable trust than in a revocable trust. Sometimes a person wanting to create a trust has confidence in the judgment and managing abilities of a relative, a friend, or a business associate. But such a person is not always available. Even if he is, he may die or become disabled or his time may be too limited.

The increasing need for reliable and capable trustees has spurred tremendous growth in the sizes and capabilities of bank trust departments and trust companies in California in recent years. Almost every bank of substantial size now has a trust department. Although their skill in managing property and investments varies, the close governmental supervision of bank trust department activities assures certain capabilities and inspires confidence in their integrity as trustees. Grantors may find the combination of an institution and an individual as co-trustees is desirable, or an individual trustee could be given some powers with others given to the institutional trustee.

Who Are the Beneficiaries?

In addition to sound financial management, a trust offers its grantor an opportunity for added flexibility in carrying out his desires regarding his beneficiaries. Many variations are available. The classic pattern is for one beneficiary to receive all of the income for life with the remainder paid at his death to another. Or income, as well as the remainder, may be divided among several beneficiaries with termination of the trust at a set time. For example, a father might create a trust providing for distribution of the income among his children until the youngest attains age 25. At that time the trust would terminate, and the principal of the trust would be divided among them as adults. The variations are limitless.

Nevertheless, one must recognize that the circumstances which inspire decisions today may change during the term of the trust. The perfect plan of distribution which is created today may become a straitjacket when unexpected events occur. A trust which irrevocably provides for the equal division of income between two children may seem unfortunate in retrospect if one child accumulates wealth and has great income and the other becomes incapacitated and incapable of supporting himself. The recognition of our inability to see into the future has given rise to several techniques for carrying out the intentions of the grantor.

Should the Trustee Have Discretion?

One method of allowing for the unexpected is to give the trustee discretion in distributing income. The trust instrument may provide that the trustee can either accumulate income in the trust or distribute it to a beneficiary depending upon the circumstances at the time. The most obvious need for such a provision is in a trust for minors. The amount of money needed for the support of a minor varies greatly as he develops through the years. Usually the decision of how much income to distribute each year can best be made as events unfold.

The grantor can specify in the instrument the criteria to be used by the trustee in making distributions. For example, the trustee may be directed to provide a standard of living comparable to that enjoyed by the beneficiary when the grantor was alive. Or, one may have sufficient confidence in the trustee to follow the often-used course of allowing the trustee complete discretion.

This same type of discretion can also be granted the trustee with respect to making distributions out of the principal of the trust as the need arises. Often the grantor will want the trustee to be able to distribute principal to one or more beneficiaries if circumstances should indicate a need. This can be arranged in the trust instrument. Guidelines can be set for such an occurrence, or it can be left up to the judgment of the trustee.

The trustee can also be granted limited or broad power to decide who among a group of beneficiaries will receive distributions of income and principal and how much they will receive. This permits making the decision at the time of distribution, rather than trying to make it in advance.

Tax Planning and Trusts

The graduated income and estate tax rates have contributed to the enormous increase in the use of trusts even for moderate estates in the past two decades. The wise use of irrevocable trusts can result in substantial savings in income and estate taxes. Often a person wishes to effect a tax savings and is also unwilling to make an outright gift to the beneficiary. Only through a trust can this person satisfy his personal preferences in making the gift and realize a tax benefit as well.

Happily for some, the program of trust planning which should be adopted without considering tax benefits is also the one which produces the greatest tax savings. For others, compromises may be necessary in weighing non-tax objectives with tax-saving techniques.

Most irrevocable trusts fall into the category of long term trusts. However a popular short term trust has been spawned almost entirely as a creature of the graduated income tax laws. Let's first take a look at the long term irrevocable trust, and then we will discuss the short term trust.

Long Term Irrevocable Trusts

Most long term irrevocable trusts are created in a will, but sometimes it is desirable to anticipate the will by making a trust during the lifetime of the grantor called an irrevocable inter vivos trust. If the trust is properly drawn, it will remove the property from the grantor's gross estate and thus effect the same tax savings as outright gifts. The grantor should reserve no right to receive income or principal from the trust, or the property will be included in his gross estate in spite of the trust gift. Furthermore, if the grantor retains too much administrative power over the trust, either as a co-trustee or otherwise, he runs the risk of losing the estate tax savings. The safest course from a tax standpoint is for the grantor to rely entirely on an independent trustee and retain no administrative power.

The Bypass Trust

Estate taxes may also be saved by avoiding the extra estate tax that results from "bunching" property in a single generation. For example, if a deceased husband leaves all his property to his wife, part or all of that property may be subject to an avoidable estate tax on his wife's death. A trust for his wife's benefit containing the portion of his property exempt from tax ($325,000 in 1984 increasing to $600,000 in 1987) can avoid the estate tax on his wife's death. Since the trust bypasses the estate tax, it is called a *bypass trust*.

The bypass trust can give the wife all the income, or distribution may be left to the discretion of the trustee. Broad flexibility is also available for distributions of principal. If the wife is the trustee, these distributions must be based on a standard related to her health, maintenance, support, and education. An independent trustee can be left complete discretion for determining distributions of principal. Whether or not the wife is trustee, she can be given a noncumulative right to receive each year a distribution up to $5,000 or 5% of principal, whichever is greater, to spend anyway she wishes without jeopardizing the ultimate tax savings.

In short, the law allows the estate planner plenty of room to tailor the trust to meet the individual needs and desires of a particular grantor without endangering the very substantial tax savings. The same rules apply regardless of which spouse dies first.

A parent may also be an ideal beneficiary of a bypass trust. If a child and a grandchild are the beneficiaries, the Generation Skipping Transfer Tax may be a consideration that should be discussed with counsel.

The Marital Deduction Trust

If a married grantor's property exceeds the amounts discussed for the bypass trust ($325,000 in 1984 increasing to $600,000 in 1987), the excess may be put in a marital deduction trust to defer all estate tax until the surviving spouse's death. The different types of marital deduction trusts should be thoroughly discussed with counsel to select the one which satisfies personal as well as financial objectives.

One of these trusts is new. It is called the *qualified terminable interest property trust,* and it allows the grantor to determine who receives the property when the surviving spouse dies. For example, if a husband wants to make sure his property passes to his children by a prior marriage on the death of his present wife, he can establish one of these trusts. His wife would receive all of the income from the trust for her life, and upon her death the property would go to his children. The wife has the benefit of the income from the trust unreduced by death taxes at the husband's death. These taxes are not paid until her death.

Of course, the surviving spouse can be given much more than just the income. She can be given as much of the principal as she requests. The properly drafted marital deduction trust can eliminate estate tax on the death of the first spouse and avoid probate on the death of the second spouse. It can be specially designed to meet family needs.

As discussed in Chapter 11, the recent removal of the limitation on the marital deduction now allows complete deferral of all estate tax until the surviving spouse's death. Many, however, have wills and trusts executed before September 13, 1981, that contain a formula that provides for the surviving spouse to receive the maximum amount then permitted under the prior limited marital deduction. If you have such a will or trust and you want your spouse and estate to have the full benefit of the new unlimited marital deduction, you must amend your will and trust after September 12, 1981, to expressly refer to an unlimited marital deduction. Otherwise, the unlimited marital deduction does not apply to your estate.

The Widow's Election Trust

This is another type of irrevocable trust that has special utility when the spouses disagree on who is to receive their property.

Though called the *widow's election trust,* it can be used by either a wife or a husband to persuade the survivor to leave his property in a certain way on his death. For example, suppose a husband and wife each have a child by a prior marriage. The wife wants the couple's property to be divided equally between the children. The husband wants the property to go only to his child. To persuade her husband, she can state in her will that if her husband puts his one half of the community property into the widow's election trust established on her death, he will receive the income from both halves of the community property for the rest of his life. Her trust would be irrevocable and would divide the property equally among the children on the husband's death. Since the offer in the wife's will is conditional, the husband must make an election. If he elects not to include his property in her trust, the income from her one half of the community will be retained in trust for the children. The special estate tax advantages of a forced widow's election merit full discussion with counsel.

The Sprinkling Trust

Income tax savings are afforded by sprinkling trusts and multiple trusts. Because of the graduated income tax rates, a given amount of income will incur the least amount of tax if it is spread among a maximum number of taxpayers. The sprinkling trust is a trust under which an independent trustee is given broad discretion to accumulate or distribute (sprinkle) income among beneficiaries. A trust of this type is a taxpayer itself, paying tax with its own income tax return on any income not distributed.

For example, suppose a man having a wife and three adult sons dies and leaves his half of the community property in three separate trusts—one for each son. The income for each trust can be accumulated or distributed either to the son for whom it is named or to the mother. The mother has the other half of the community property. If her property proves inadequate for her support, the income from the trusts can be distributed to her. If she has adequate funds, then the income can be retained in the trusts where it will be taxed in a lower bracket, or some or all of it can be distributed to the sons if they need it. They may also be in a low tax bracket. The income is divided among the mother, the three trusts, and the three sons—seven taxpayers—so as to provide maximum tax advantages subject to the throwback rule while taking care of their needs.

In creating long term trusts, the grantor should take care in selecting the trustee and in providing for successor trustees. The trustee or trustees should be given broad enough management and investment powers to permit flexible administration of the trust in today's complex economic environment.

Short Term Trusts

Our high, graduated income tax rates have given rise to a specialized type of short term trust designed primarily to shift the income tax burden to a lower tax bracket. It is sometimes called a Clifford Trust.

A good example is the executive whose income falls partly in the top 50% income tax bracket. He is supporting his elderly, widowed mother who lives modestly and comfortably on $10,000 per year. In order to provide that $10,000 per year after taxes of 50%, the executive must produce $20,000 in income. If he could put income producing property into trust for his mother so that the income would go directly to her and would be taxed at her own low income tax bracket instead of his, the savings would be startling. By shifting property generating only about $11,000 of taxable income to her, he could provide her with the after-tax income of approximately $10,000. This means about $11,000 of income would provide for his mother what had been requiring $20,000.

Happily, the tax law allows this type of savings if the rules are followed. The first essential is that the trust must be for ten years if the property is to come back to the grantor at its termination. It can alternatively be made to terminate at the death of the income beneficiary (the mother in our example), regardless of the life expectancy of that beneficiary.

Since this type of short term trust is not aimed at saving estate taxes, considerably more power can be retained by the grantor than with the long term irrevocable trust. He can even be the trustee if the trust is drawn so as to prohibit his exercising certain prohibited powers generally related to distribution of income and principal of the trust. The grantor can reserve the right to determine how much of the income will be distributed to the beneficiary from time to time, so long as any undistributed income is allowed to accumulate in the trust to be distributed to the beneficiary when the trust terminates.

The support of an elderly dependent mother is only one example. Children, grandchildren, other relatives, and even nonrelatives may be beneficiaries. The trusts may be an excellent way to save money for a child's college education. However, if minor children are beneficiaries of a trust created by their parent, care must be taken to assure that the income is not used to satisfy the parent's legal obligation to support the minor children. Any trust income so used will be taxed to the grantor.

Finally, it should be pointed out that a grantor need not be in the 50% bracket. Many such trusts allow substantial income tax savings for taxpayers whose top bracket is much lower.

Summary

Irrevocable trusts, created either while living or by will, are extremely useful estate planning tools, both for tax and nontax reasons. Large savings in both estate taxes and income taxes can be realized; but even more important, proper management of property and provisions for effective security for one's family can often be assured only through trusts.

14
Should I Make Gifts to Charity?

Charitable donations have become an accepted and sometimes expected part of today's society. Individual contributions, compared to corporate or foundation grants, compose almost 90% of the $53 billion raised for philanthropy in 1981. The decision to make gifts to charity, either during one's lifetime or by will, is a personal matter. Obviously, the selection of the charity, the timing, the amount, and the type of property given will depend upon the individual's attitude, desires, financial resources, and responsibilities.

Once the decision has been made to contribute to charity, or at least to consider it, the tax effects of the gift become important; income, gift, and estate tax deductions are allowable for certain charitable gifts. Often, income taxes are the largest item of an individual's budget, and in many instances, the estate tax bill is the largest expense of the deceased's estate. If a person can accomplish his charitable objectives and reduce his tax bill, he is apt to be a "cheerful giver."

Gifts of Cash or Property

When considering some sort of charitable contribution by will, most people think in terms of a cash bequest of a fixed amount with the bulk of the estate passing to the surviving family. Under such circumstances the entire amount of the charitable bequest is usually deductible for federal estate tax purposes.

Often, however, cash will be needed in the estate to defray costs of administration and taxes. Payment of the charitable legacies in cash could produce a cash shortage, necessitating the sale of other properties. The estate may be composed primarily of real estate or closely held corporate stocks, which may be non-liquid in the sense that they cannot be sold easily. Sale of those properties either to pay the charitable cash bequest or to restore the cash used to pay the charity may not only be inconvenient but may result in an income tax if the property sold has appreciated in value between the date of the decedent's death and the time of the sale. To avoid these problems, the individual may wish to leave property to charity in his will instead of cash. The entire value of the property given will usually be estate tax deductible.

Fixed Amount or Percentage

Instead of giving a specific dollar amount or designated properties to charity, one may wish to consider giving a fixed percentage of his estate. If the will is drafted so that administrative costs of the estate do not come out of the gift, the entire gift will be deductible for federal estate tax purposes. Another advantage of the percentage gift is an across-the-board reduction of the gift if the estate has a lower value than the donor expected.

Trust Gifts

Family responsibilities may prevent a substantial outright gift by will to charity. However, family circumstances may make it possible to make a charitable gift in trust of the income or of the remainder in certain properties. For example, a person may wish to provide a life income to his spouse or to his parents with the property ultimately passing to charity. Or he may feel that adequate provision has been made for his children during their minority and arrange for the income from the property to be paid to charity until the children become adults at which time they will receive the property.

Under either arrangement the present value of the charity's income interest or remainder interest would be deductible for estate tax purposes if the trust included a number of safeguards in order for the charity's interest to be well defined. In our example where the spouse or parents received income for life, the trust could be a *charitable remainder unitrust* or a *charitable remainder annuity trust*. In our example where the charity received the income until the children were adults, the trust would be a *charitable lead trust*. The elimination of all estate tax while satisfying family and charitable objectives is not uncommon and should be discussed with counsel.

Lifetime Gifts

If a person has decided to make charitable contributions, it may be appropriate to consider making them while still living. Lifetime outright gifts and any subsequent appreciation in their value, of course, are eliminated from the donor's estate. Their values are completely deductible for gift tax purposes, and unlike most charitable gifts made by will, lifetime gifts to charities may result in an income tax deduction to the donor.

For example, if a person wishes to give certain property to charity at his death, it may be desirable for him to establish a trust during his lifetime, reserving an income interest for himself for life with the remainder going to charity at his death. Since the only gift is that of the remainder interest and it is given to charity, there would be no gift tax. The value of the property in the trust has not been removed from the donor's estate for estate tax purposes because the income was reserved for life. However, since the property will pass to charity at his death, it will be deductible from the gross estate. Moreover, the value of the remainder interest given to charity is deductible for income tax purposes providing safeguards for defining the charity's interest are included in the form of a charitable remainder annuity trust or unitrust.

The amount of the income tax deduction varies with the length of time the charity must wait for the gift, but the deduction is immediate so that spendable dollars in the year of the gift are increased. The income interest is paid to the donor for the rest of his life.

Under such arrangement properties which have appreciated in value since the donor acquired them may be given to the trust. It is better to contribute these appreciated properties to the trust and obtain a higher income tax charitable deduction than to sell the properties, pay the capital gain tax and contribute the remaining proceeds to the trust.

Income Tax Deduction for Gifts

There are limitations on the amount of charitable gifts that are tax deductible within a given year. Generally, charitable contributions to public charities are deductible up to 50% of the contribution base, which is adjusted gross income subject to certain adjustments. Contributions to certain charitable foundations, on the other hand, are deductible up to only 20% of the contribution base. The size of the charitable contribution in any particular year must be carefully planned if all of it is to be tax deductible. The excess of a charitable donation to a public charity over the income tax limitations can be deducted in the five following years. Alternatively, the donations can be made over a period of years. Thus, rather than giving a block of stock in one particular year, a smaller number of shares might be given over several years. Similarly, undivided interests in real estate can be given periodically to maximize available income tax benefits.

Gifts of Life Insurance

There are, of course, other methods of making charitable contributions. One of these involves using life insurance. An individual may transfer to charity an existing life insurance policy and be entitled to a charitable deduction based on the value of the policy. Subsequent premium payments will also be deductible for income tax purposes. If the donor keeps the policy but names the charity beneficiary, the proceeds are includable in his estate but deductible as an estate tax charitable deduction.

Charitable Foundations

If the donor wishes to make substantial gifts to charity, he might consider establishing his own charitable foundation. Usually an individual establishes a foundation in the form of a non-profit corporation. A ruling is obtained from the Internal Revenue Service. Subsequent gifts to the foundation are deductible for income, gift, and estate tax purposes, and the income of the foundation, with certain restrictions, is tax free.

The individual or his family usually controls the investment and donation policies of the foundation. The foundation makes investments which are almost entirely tax free and also makes grants to other charities. The individuals can thereby maximize their potential for charitable giving. Their foundation will memorialize their name as well as any cause they may be supporting. It can introduce their children to the importance their parents place on charitable giving. Charitable foundations are subject to complex rules and restrictions so care must be exercised in their creation and operation in order to maintain the exemption from tax.

Gift of Remainder Interest in Personal Residence

A donor may wish to contribute the remainder interest in his personal residence, farm, vacation home, or stock in a cooperative apartment used as a residence. The donor retains the right to live in his residence or use it for a term of years or for the rest of his life and the life of his spouse. The donor is entitled to an immediate income tax deduction based on the value of the remainder interest in the residence contributed to charity.

Pooled Income Funds

These are similar in concept to mutual funds. They are offered by many charities in California. A donor contributes generally cash or securities to the fund and receives his pro rata share of the fund's income for the rest of his life. Upon his death his share of the fund is then given to the charity. He not only receives an immediate charitable income tax deduction but also avoids any tax on the appreciation in any securities contributed. The fund managers diversify the fund's investments and maximize the return. A pooled income fund permits a donor with highly appreciated but low yielding stock to diversify and increase his income while paying no tax on the capital gain and receiving a current income tax deduction.

Gift Annuities

Many charities are licensed in California to sell gift annuities. The donor transfers money or property to the charity in exchange for the annuity. He receives a guaranteed fixed sum usually monthly, commencing either immediately or at a future date and continuing for the rest of his life and the life of his spouse. The donor receives a charitable income tax deduction and favored treatment on any capital gain in the property transferred to the charity.

Gift annuities can be obtained, for example, in exchange for the remainder interest in a home. The donor continues to live in his home and receives a monthly check from the charity for the rest of his life.

Summary

The manner in which charitable gifts can be most advantageously utilized by the individual depends on the amount and nature of his assets and the relationship of the income, gift, and estate taxes to his own particular situation. Apart from tax advantages, charitable giving often makes good sense for family reasons. Coordination of charitable contributions with plans for individual or family estate planning often results in maximizing one's charitable and personal objectives.

15
Probate and Tax Savings Through Gifts

Gifts play a part in passing property from one generation to the next, even where there is no professional "estate planner" involved. Farmers and ranchers often give their children a few head of livestock so that they may acquire experience in animal husbandry or have an opportunity to build a herd of their own over the years. Parents may transfer an interest in the family business to a child in order to increase the child's interest in the enterprise and prepare him or her to assume the responsibilities of management. One spouse will often place securities in trust to assure income for the other spouse. Parents may do the same for the protection of their children.

Gifts Avoid Probate

Gifts reduce income and death taxes as well as lower the costs of probate. In planning gifts, however, the welfare of the person making the gift and the welfare of the one receiving it should be paramount considerations. An older person should not make gifts which would impair his security, his capacity to provide for himself, or his opportunity to continue useful and gainful employment. A child should not be given funds or property which the child is too young to handle. The selection and timing of gifts to young people who lack experience in financial management should be designed to further their proper training and development with adequate provisions for the care and management of property. A desire to effect a tax savings or to avoid probate costs should be secondary considerations. It is better to provide for the payment of taxes and other costs by additional life insurance or some other method than to make gifts which would prejudice the security of the donor or be unsuited to the position of the recipient.

There are a number of different ways that gifts may be made. If gifts are made to a minor or to an incompetent, a guardian or conservator may have to be appointed by the Superior Court to administer the estate of the recipient. Statutes have been enacted under which gifts may be made to a "custodian" who holds the property for a minor. In addition, gifts may be made in one of the various types of trusts that we discussed in Chapters 10 and 13.

Guardianships

Gifts which come under the administration of guardians or conservators often result in legal problems and therefore may not be desirable. Guardianship laws are designed to provide the maximum protection for the child. They require periodic court accountings and may require the guardian to post a bond. Both these and other provisions may occasion expense and complications. A guardian or conservator is severely restricted in investing the ward's funds without court authorization. Such management is inflexible, cumbersome, and may be expensive as well.

Custodial Arrangements

The California Uniform Gifts to Minors Act is designed to provide a simple way by which property may be acquired for a minor. It contains provisions for custody, reinvestment, and disbursement by the custodian on behalf of a minor. The custodian does not have to post a bond. While the procedure for establishing a custodial arrangement is comparatively simple, the family and tax consequences should be discussed with counsel.

There are some disadvantages in the use of custodians. When a person names himself custodian for another, as in the case of a father for his child, the property given still remains within the gross estate of the donor (the father) for estate tax purposes. The custodial property must all be given to the minor on reaching age eighteen regardless of the minor's maturity or ability to handle the property.

Gifts in Trust

The gift in trust is the generally accepted method of making indirect gifts where a direct gift is inappropriate. In almost every case a gift in trust is preferable to a gift to a custodian or guardian. In a trust the donor can specify the rules to be applied to the management and use of the property. The terms of the trust may be more or less restrictive than a custodianship or guardianship, and provisions may be inserted for many eventualities. An individual, bank, or trust company may serve as a trustee. Whether the legal expenses involved in the establishment and operation of a trust will be greater or less than those involved in a guardianship or conservatorship covering the same amount of property depends on the particular situation involved. In any individual case, however, the alternative advantages and disadvantages of various methods of making gifts will involve legal issues on which competent advice can be obtained only from an attorney who is familiar with trust matters. (See Chapters 10 and 13.)

Gift Tax Considerations

The federal gift tax is imposed on gratuitous transfers by an individual during life as opposed to the federal estate tax which is imposed on the taxable estate transferred at death. Though they are separate taxes, they are integrated under a single rate table, which determines the amount of the tax, and unified credit, which determines how much of the tax has to be paid.

The federal gift tax is imposed on a calendar year basis at graduated rates upon the taxable gifts made during the year. The federal gift tax is cumulative. This means that the total taxable gifts made in prior years is added to the taxable gifts for the current year to determine the gift tax rate applicable to the current year's taxable gifts.

Not all gifts result in a federal gift tax. Certain charitable gifts are deductible as are gifts made to one's spouse or for medical care or tuition. We will discuss each of these types of deductible gifts later in the chapter. There is a deduction for gifts made to third parties in which the spouse joins (gift-splitting). Gift-splitting applies only to separate property or quasi-community property and not to community property.

The "annual exclusion" discussed in the next section permits the first $10,000 of present interest gifts made to each donee during a calendar year to be gift tax free.

Furthermore, a federal unified gift and estate tax credit is allowed against gift tax liability on gifts made on or after January 1, 1977. This credit is phased in over a number of years, and the total amount of gifts which may be made during a donor's lifetime without tax, but which will reduce the amount of property that will pass free from estate tax upon a donor's death, is as follows:

1983	$275,000
1984	325,000
1985	400,000
1986	500,000
1987 and thereafter	600,000

The person making the gift (the donor) is primarily liable for the gift tax, though the recipient may become liable if the donor defaults in the payment of the gift tax. It is also possible to make what is known as a "net gift" in which the donee of the gift agrees to become responsible for the payment of the gift tax, which in turn reduces the amount of the gift and any gift tax reportable by the donor.

Generally gifts are not includable in the gross estate for death tax purposes. There are, however, several exceptions to this rule. One is gifts of life insurance if the transfer of the insurance was within three years of the donor's death. Another is gifts with certain "retained interests" or those over which the donor retains a "general power of appointment" as we discussed in Chapter 11.

In light of the unification of federal gift and estate tax, is there still any tax advantage to making lifetime gifts? Yes. First, any appreciation attributable to the gifted property after the date of the gift will not be includable in the gross estate unless the transfer violates one of the rules referred to previously. If property is given away early enough, the appreciation can amount to many times the initial value of the property at the time of the gift. Second, any gift tax paid with respect to the gifted property, if made more than three years before the decedent's death, will also not be in the gross estate of the decedent. In a highly inflationary economy, the ability to pass substantial amounts of appreciation to a second generation may mean the difference between the ability to keep a family farm, business, or other valuable assets and the necessity of having to dispose of them, perhaps in a distress sale.

The Annual Exclusion

The annual exclusion provision permits a person to make a tax free gift of cash or property worth up to $10,000 to each of any number of people each year.

It was created to exclude normal periodic gifts, such as wedding and Christmas presents. A single person wishing to give a total of $30,000 each year gift tax free can do so if he divides the gifts equally among three recipients. However, to qualify for the annual exclusion, a gift must be one of a "present interest," which is the right to absolute, immediate enjoyment of the gift.

A gift to a revocable trust is not deemed a completed gift, since it is revocable. Therefore no gift tax is due. On the other hand, a gift to an irrevocable trust, is a completed gift. But the irrevocable trust must contain special provisions for the gift to convey a present interest to the beneficiary and thereby qualify for the annual exclusion.

Three common examples of the irrevocable trusts that qualify for the annual exclusion are:

1. An irrevocable "minor's trust" that requires income and principal to be distributed for the benefit of the minor until age twenty-one with the balance then given to him outright upon his reaching majority.
2. An irrevocable trust that provides the beneficiary with a right to withdraw the annual gifts to the trust or the annual exclusion, whichever is less.
3. An irrevocable trust that requires all income to be paid currently to the income beneficiary. In this case, the income interest is a present interest and qualifies for the annual exclusion.

Since a husband and wife may combine their exclusions, as much as $20,000 can be given to each recipient each year. For example, a married couple owning substantial amounts of corporate stock and having four children could give $80,000 worth of stock to their children each year. Over a period of twenty years they could give gift tax free $1,600,000 worth of stock. Allowing for ordinary appreciation, the amount removed from their estate might be substantially greater when valued at the end of the twenty-year period. The power of a husband and wife to combine their exclusions applies even though the property given is separate property (the "gift-splitting" referred to earlier).

Gifts for Medical and Tuition Expenses

Payments for school tuition or medical expenses may also be made free from gift tax. The payments must be after 1981 and must be made directly to the school or the one providing the medical care.

Charitable and Other Deductible Gifts

No gift tax is paid on contributions to charity. Such gifts are deducted in computing the amount of taxable gifts reported in a calendar year. Special rules apply for deducting gifts of income or remainder interests in trust to charities. (See Chapter 14.)

The Gift Tax Marital Deduction

No gift tax is paid on gifts from one spouse to another. These gifts are also deducted in computing the amount of taxable gifts reported in a calendar year. The gift of a life estate or terminable interest to a spouse does not ordinarily qualify for the marital deduction. However, if it is one of "qualified terminable interest property," then the gift will qualify for the unlimited gift tax marital deduction. (See Chapters 11 and 13.)

How the Tax Is Calculated

The federal gift tax is computed on a cumulative basis. When taxable gifts are made, the amount of the gift tax is determined by adding the total taxable gifts made in the current and prior years and subtracting the gift tax paid or unified credit used. For this reason gift tax brackets increase as taxable gifts are made.

> Example: A husband who had made no previous gifts made gifts of $150,000 of his separate property to his wife and $100,000 of his separate property to his son in the calendar year 1983. Both gifts qualify for the $10,000 annual exclusion and the spouse may elect to split the husband's gift to the son.

The husband's gift tax for 1983 is computed as follows:

1. Total gifts for year	$250,000
2. Less: One half of the son's gift attributable to wife	50,000
3. Husband's gifts	200,000
4. Less total annual exclusions on gifts to son and wife	20,000
5. Gifts reduced by exclusions	180,000
6. Less marital deduction	140,000*
7. Taxable gifts	40,000
8. Tax before credit on $40,000	8,200
9. Less unused unified credit	8,200
10. Tax due	$ 0

* $150,000 less $10,000 annual exclusion

Primary Considerations in Making a Gift

If property given in trust is to be removed from the gross estate of the donor for federal estate tax purposes, the gift must be irrevocable, and the donor must part with the right to receive income from the gift. The donor must forego the right to determine how trust benefits are shared among the beneficiaries. Although the donor may be the trustee, it is usually desirable to utilize an independent trustee to avoid estate taxes. The variations which satisfy tax requirements are numerous, and the controlling rules are technical. Therefore, the lawyer must develop a recommendation in each case which will comply with such rules while fulfilling family needs.

A variety of more specialized devices may be considered in larger estates where federal estate tax problems are especially critical. It may be helpful to combine a gift with a sale of property to one's children by selling them property which has appreciated in value at its original cost. The parent will ordinarily realize no taxable gain from the sale, and the amount of the gift will be the value of the property over the sale price. Property may be sold to children or others for its actual value with the purchase price payable in installments. The payment of the installments may be forgiven or cancelled as they become due. This approach is more practical where there has been no substantial appreciation in the value of the property from the time it was acquired.

Special types of gifts may be desirable to permit a wife or child to carry insurance on the life of the father. This situation may enable the family to keep the insurance from being taxable for federal estate tax purposes at the father's death and still have the funds available. As we will discuss in the next chapter, the life insurance trust is a common vehicle for meeting family needs in this area.

Where larger amounts of property are involved, other types of special arrangements may be required. It may be desirable to change the form of organization of the parent's business to create interests which are easily transferred by gift. For example, a sole proprietorship or partnership might be incorporated, or voting rights in stock in a family enterprise may be modified so that shares are created which are appropriate for gift purposes. In such circumstances special consideration must be given to the effect which such stock provisions may have on the valuation of the shares. Estate freezing techniques may be applied which may shift appreciation out of the parent's gross estate. Each situation presents different problems, and there are no ready-made solutions. For this reason the development of an appropriate solution in any individual case should take into consideration the economic and tax positions of the parties, the proper management of the property and above all the best interests of the persons involved.

16
Life Insurance

Ownership of life insurance is another method of transferring wealth to family and other heirs without the necessity of formal probate or the use of a will. It is, no doubt, one of the most commonly held and yet widely misunderstood assets.

The Concept

By and large, the general concept of life insurance is easy to understand. An insurance company (*insurer*) agrees with an individual (*insured*) to pay a sum of money, in one lump sum or over time, at that person's death, whenever it occurs. The proceeds of the policy will be distributed directly to the beneficiary by virtue of the contractual obligation of the insurer, rather than through any other dispositive instrument of the insured like his will.

In exchange, the insured agrees to pay a periodic payment (*premium*) to the insurer in an amount which is mathematically and actuarially calculated to be sufficient to cover the death benefit, administration and overhead costs, commissions, and profits. The insurance company attempts to predict when its insureds are likely to die, how much profit they can make with each insured's premium payments over the years before his death and the costs associated with administering the system. This, coupled with favorable tax laws on insurance company reserves, enables the insurer to provide substantial proceeds to the beneficiaries of the insured even if the individual dies shortly after taking out the policy.

The owner of the policy (*policyholder*) is often, but not necessarily, the insured. Sometimes the policyholder is also the beneficiary, or the beneficiary is a trust established for the benefit of the insured's family or heirs. The policyholder has the obligation to make the premium payments as well as the power to decide, among other things, who the beneficiary will be, how the proceeds will be paid, and whether to borrow any cash value in the policy.

Types of Policies

Describing the types of insurance policies available today would require a full length book. Even then the description is apt to be incomplete, since new policies are continually being introduced.

There are two primary categories of insurance contracts, with numerous variations available. They are *ordinary* life and *term* life insurance. An ordinary life insurance policy is a permanent contract with an even (nonincreasing) cost to the purchaser based upon the age of the insured at the time the policy is first acquired. The insurer establishes a fixed price which contains a cost for the increasing risk of mortality and a cost for the savings portion of the policy, known as cash surrender value or just cash value. The cash value portion is the excess charge which affords the insured the right to a level premium payment.

Some ordinary life products require premium payments continually until death. Others are designed to be fully paid up at a specific age (for example, at age 65). In recent years, the cash value of some policies has been capable of growing so rapidly through interest allocated or dividends paid by the insurer that the incremental value is sufficient to actually pay the next year's policy premium.

A term life insurance policy is a limited duration contract which lasts only as long as the term prescribed plus any extensions or renewals. The term can vary usually from one to five years. The contract can provide for automatic renewal, discretionary renewal, or nonrenewal. Typically, the cost of these policies increases with each renewal as the risk of the insured's mortality increases. Since there is usually no cash value associated with these policies, the initial cost is substantially reduced. Ultimately the premium cost of the term policy will exceed the cost of the permanent policy. Whether the full contract price is cheaper with term insurance or permanent insurance depends on many factors including the insured's age and mortality, the cost of money, the tax treatment of the premium payment, the policy proceeds, and the various policy provisions.

Tax Treatment of Life Insurance

There are a variety of income, gift, and estate tax consequences that affect the purchase, ownership, and transfer of insurance policies and the receipt of policy proceeds upon the death of the insured.

How is the beneficiary taxed upon receipt of life insurance proceeds? Generally, the proceeds payable by reason of an insured's death are not subject to income tax whether paid to individual beneficiaries or to the insured's estate. There may be tax, however, if the proceeds are paid to one who holds the policy as collateral security or if the policy is sold prior to the insured's death or where the proceeds are received as alimony.

What if the insurance proceeds are paid over a fixed period of time or in a fixed amount in installments? The proceeds are still exempt from income tax while any interest attributable to the installments is taxable as ordinary income subject to a special $1,000 annual exclusion for interest payments to a surviving spouse. This exclusion should especially be examined by surviving spouses in higher income tax brackets to maximize their return.

Are premium payments deductible by the policyholder or taxable to him? A policy owned by an individual is considered a personal asset, and premium payments are deemed nondeductible personal expenses. Premiums paid by someone other than a policyholder, such as a parent, child, or friend, is considered a gift to the owner rather than income.

Premiums paid by an employer on a policy owned by an employee is considered taxable compensation to him, unless it is part of a special plan of group term insurance.

Premium payments for insurance that is part of such a group plan, or purchased in a qualified retirement plan, may create some taxable income to the insured employee and some nontaxable income.

Will the proceeds of life insurance be subject to federal estate tax? If insurance proceeds are paid to or for the benefit of the insured's estate, the proceeds will be included in his gross estate and subject to death taxes. Where the insured retained at his death any "incidents of ownership" over the policy, the proceeds will also be included in his gross estate. The phrase "incidents of ownership" has specific meaning in the tax law. It refers to such powers as the right to designate the beneficiary, to determine the time and manner of payment of proceeds, to borrow on the cash surrender value, and to transfer such ownership interest to someone else.

An insurance policy which is transferred to a third party by the insured within three years of his death is automatically included in the insured's estate. The reason for the transfer is irrelevant; the only issue is whether the transfer took place within three years of death. If so, the entire policy proceeds are included in the gross estate for estate tax purposes.

Are there any gift taxes required upon the transfer of a life insurance policy or gratuitous payment of premiums? A gift of an insurance policy occurs when the policyholder irrevocably transfers all incidents of ownership to a third party for less than full and adequate consideration. If the transfer is revocable or the donor retains incidents of ownership, then the gift is incomplete for gift tax purposes. It does not mean that the donee has no power over the policy transferred, only that a taxable gift has not occurred.

An insurance policy is valued at its fair market value as of the time of the gift. Such value will vary depending on the type of policy involved. An ordinary life policy is measured by its "interpolated terminal reserve value," roughly equivalent to its cash surrender value plus any unearned premiums. A term life policy is usually worth only the amount of any unearned premiums.

Where the gift is made of current or future premiums, the value is equal to the premiums paid.

Gifts of insurance are entitled to the $10,000 per donee annual exclusion, as long as the donee received a present interest in the gift.

Where a policy is gifted to a spouse, it is entitled to the unlimited marital deduction. In other words, no tax would be due though a return may have to be filed.

Life Insurance Trust

Frequently, an individual desires to acquire a life insurance policy on himself providing for his heirs at his death but is concerned that the proceeds will be poorly managed, available to the creditors of the beneficiaries, or subject to death tax in his estate or that of a beneficiary. In these cases, the insured may elect to create a trust to own or acquire such a policy and to receive the proceeds upon his death.

As discussed in Chapters 10 and 13, such trusts can be "revocable" or "irrevocable," depending on the purpose and planning objectives of the insured. In recent years, it has become very popular to establish irrevocable insurance trusts for the benefit of the spouse for life and then for the children at the spouse's death. Under this arrangement, an insured creates a trust that is irrevocable and therefore cannot be amended. An independent trustee (friend, advisor, trust officer, etc.) is named to manage the trust, which is funded only with an insurance policy (or policies) and enough cash to pay the initial premium. Each year, additional cash gifts are made to fund the current year's premium obligation.

The trust provides that, at the death of the insured, the policy proceeds will be held by the trustee for the benefit of the noninsured spouse. Income is paid periodically to her, and principal is available for her health, support, and maintenance. The trust can purchase assets from the insured's estate or the spouse in order to increase liquidity to pay taxes or cover living expenses.

When the spouse dies, the remaining proceeds can be distributed outright to the children or held in trust until the children reach sufficient age and maturity to responsibly handle their portion of the funds. Again, the trust can purchase assets from the noninsured spouse's estate, so that the estate would have sufficient cash to pay death taxes without having to sell assets to outside third parties.

The unique tax advantages of this device include avoiding death tax when the insured dies (since he gifted the policy away to the irrevocable trust, presumably more than three years before death) as well as when the noninsured spouse dies (since she is treated as never owning the policy or controlling the trust). Moreover, the costs and delays of probate are avoided on the deaths of both spouses as well as on the death of any child dying before the age set for outright distribution.

Summary

The absence of any death taxes, income taxes, or significant gift taxes on the insurance policy proceeds makes the irrevocable life insurance trust an attractive planning tool. But such advantages are available only to a carefully designed and artfully drafted instrument. Community property rules do not prevent, but may certainly complicate, an effective plan.

17
Planning for Disability: The New Durable Power of Attorney

Wills are designed to assist you in planning affairs for the years that follow your death. In the many years that precede death, there is a danger you may suffer a physical or mental disability (or both) which may last for months or years. Such disabilities can be significant enough to prevent you from handling your personal and business matters and from making even day-to-day decisions.

What documents can be used during such disability to assist in handling these matters? The revocable trust discussed in Chapter 10 can provide for a successor trustee to serve in the event of your incapacity. California law now provides for a durable power of attorney and since January 1, 1984 also makes special provision for a durable power of attorney for health care.

What Is a Durable Power of Attorney?

Many people are familiar with the phrase "power of attorney." Banks, insurance companies, and lawyers often use the general *non-durable* power of attorney for you to appoint another as your attorney in fact to make decisions, sign documents, handle financial transactions, and sell real estate, stock, and other property on your behalf.

California law permits you to authorize another to do with few limitations any acts that you might do directly. This is the law of agency and has been a part of the Anglo-American legal system for hundreds of years.

However, the nondurable power of attorney has one very serious problem. The moment the authorizing person (called the *principal*) becomes incapacitated, the nondurable power of attorney automatically terminates. The appointed person (called the *attorney in fact*) then no longer has the power to act on behalf of his principal. At the very moment when he could be most useful in writing checks, making business decisions, and taking other steps on behalf of his principal, the attorney in fact has lost his power to do so.

The durable power of attorney solves this problem by continuing the authority of the attorney in fact *indefinitely* after the incapacity or disability of the principal until the principal's death.

What Makes a Power of Attorney Durable?

The durable power of attorney must contain words showing the principal's intent that the authority conferred is exercisable in spite of the principal's becoming incapacitated. The words suggested in the law are "This power of attorney shall not be affected by subsequent incapacity of the principal" or "This power of attorney shall become effective upon the incapacity of the principal." Therefore, you may designate when a durable power of attorney becomes effective. The durable power of attorney may be immediately effective, or it may become effective only upon the principal's incapacity. In the latter event the authority of the attorney in fact does not begin until the principal becomes incapacitated.

The new durable power of attorney can be specifically drafted to fit individual needs and should be fully discussed with your attorney as a valuable part of your estate plan. One version or another of the "durable power" is now in effect in at least forty states, but the law is relatively new in California.

Medical Treatment and Personal Care Decisions

California has a court-supervised procedure for persons who are not capable of taking care of themselves medically or personally or of handling their business and financial affairs. If the incapacitated person is an adult, the court appoints someone who is known as the conservator to handle those matters for that person. The incapacitated person is called the conservatee.

Getting a conservator appointed is both time consuming and expensive. The new durable power of attorney offers an adult another way of appointing a legal representative without going to court. In any event, you may in a durable power of attorney also nominate a conservator of your person or your estate or both. The court considers this nomination if someone starts a conservatorship court action.

With a durable power of attorney for health care, you may appoint an attorney in fact who can execute your wishes as to the kind of medical treatment you prefer if you are later unable to give informed consent for health care decisions. The treatment may range from maximum care (including extraordinary life-support equipment) to minimum care. Your particular religious or personal preferences can be specifically set forth in the durable power of attorney. These may give additional guidance when you have executed a document making a gift of a part of your body for transplantation or scientific purposes or where you have executed a "Directive to Physicians" under the Natural Death Act.

In addition to helping the disabled person with medical decisions, the attorney in fact appointed under the durable power of attorney for health care can be authorized to sign hospital forms. The attorney in fact may obtain information about the principal's physical and mental condition to find out whether he is disabled and to assist the doctors for the principal with decisions about care.

The attorney in fact can be given a durable power to employ and discharge a wide variety of persons (including professionals such as doctors, dentists, and private duty nurses), to select the place where the principal will live, to arrange for care and support of the principal's children, parents, or other dependents, to handle the principal's mail, to make decisions about the principal's recreational, spiritual, and other activities, and similar powers.

Property Management and Financial Planning Decisions

While the principal is disabled or incapacitated, the attorney in fact can handle an almost limitless number of business and financial matters. For example, he can be given a durable power to write checks, pay bills, sell real estate and personal property, operate a business, deal with retirement plans, borrow money, buy new property, handle life insurance matters, cancel credit cards, gain access to the principal's safe deposit box, and take custody of personal records.

If the principal is unlikely to recover from the disability, the attorney in fact may be empowered to take certain steps which the principal can no longer do in anticipation of death, including some of the very estate planning ideas discussed in other chapters of this book. While he cannot sign a new will for the principal, he can work with the principal's attorney to transfer assets to his living trust, make charitable and other gifts, sign documents, and do other things which may reduce the estate tax and otherwise accomplish the wishes of the principal.

Who Should Be Selected as an Attorney in Fact Under a Durable Power?

There are many persons who might serve well as an attorney in fact under either type of durable power of attorney. Those closest to you (spouse, close relative, significant personal friend) might be best to handle the personal care and medical treatment decisions. You might also think of clergymen in that connection if they would be preferable. Business associates might do well in handling business and property matters, as long as they will not have a conflict of interest at some later date in a decision that has to be made.

It is not only possible but usually preferable to create two different documents: one durable power for health care for one attorney in fact to handle personal care and medical treatment decisions and a separate durable power with a different attorney in fact to handle the estate planning, property, and financial matters.

The important considerations are:

1. Is the person selected willing to serve over an undetermined period of time?
2. Does that person know you well and your beliefs, values, preferences, and opinions?
3. Will he want to be paid for his time in handling your affairs?

Language in the durable power can protect him from legal liability for any of his actions except actions done to cheat you or similar wrongdoing. It is an important responsibility with which to trust another person, and selections of an attorney in fact should be made with great care. That person will have enormous control over your life and assets.

Will the Authority of the Attorney in Fact Be Accepted by Others?

This is a new concept in California. As with any new law, institutions such as banks, hospitals, and governmental bodies may be unsure of what the law does allow until a court has held in a specific case the extent of the new law's provisions. Thus, it may take several years to find out exactly what powers can be given to an attorney in fact and respected by third persons under a durable power. However, the concept has been accepted in most other states and is likely to be well received by California courts.

Summary

While normally you have the right to revoke or cancel a durable power, it is important to understand that during a time of disability it may be too late to change your mind. Therefore, the careful selection of provisions as well as of the attorney in fact should be done with advice of counsel in order to safely obtain the full benefits of these new powers.

18

Joint Tenancy and Tenancy in Common: A Warning

There may be more misinformation about the law of joint tenancy than about any other subject in the law. The best advice for you is to seek advice from your lawyer before you create a joint tenancy ownership of property with anyone. A small checking or savings account in joint tenancy with your spouse may be satisfactory, but beyond that, be warned: Creation of a joint tenancy without careful consideration can have expensive tax results and place the ultimate ownership of the property in unexpected hands. Actually, if a law were passed in California to void all joint tenancies created by persons without advice of an attorney, many family disputes, much litigation, and expensive tax traps could be eliminated.

Here is a simple case as an illustration: Mr. and Mrs. Jones took title to their home as joint tenants. The deed read, "Arthur Jones and Mary Jones, his wife, as joint tenants." The home cost $50,000 thirty years ago. Its present market value is $325,000. Should either die, the survivor will sell the home. Should title remain in joint tenancy? That depends upon many things. If it remains in joint tenancy and Mr. Jones dies and his widow sells the home, a capital gains tax might result that could have been saved by placing the home in their names as community property. The word "might" is used advisedly. Without full knowledge of the facts and the law, an advisor cannot make a proper recommendation in this case. Whose funds were used to purchase the home? Were the funds separate, community, or quasi-community funds? Would probate or confirmation costs be increased needlessly if title to the property were changed? What gift taxes, income taxes, and death taxes could result? What happens to the property on the death of the surviving spouse?

Origin

Many people believe that an ideal method of owning property is "joint tenancy with right of survivorship." The ownership of property with right of survivorship is not a new idea. If two or more persons bought property and had title taken in both names, the presumption was that they intended to own it with right of survivorship. So, if land was sold to Doe and to Smith and if neither sold his interest prior to the death of the other, then when one died, his 50% interest in the land also died, and the survivor owned 100%. This was their implied agreement.

From a practical standpoint, the chief characteristic of joint tenancy is the survivor gets the decedent's interest automatically. Its appealing aspect is the saving of time and expense by avoiding probate.

In time this chief characteristic lost its appeal, partly because of the abolition of early feudal taxes and partly because it became less desirable to have the ultimate ownership depend on the chance of survival. The owner of a joint interest could not dispose of it by his will. Even if he had a will that specifically gave the land to his children, his interest would not automatically go to his children. If a joint tenant wanted his interest to pass at his death to somebody other than his joint tenant, he had to break the joint tenancy while both joint tenants were alive.

Tenancy In Common

During common law development over the centuries favoring the right of survivorship changed to favoring tenancy in common. If Jones and Fox buy land together today, it is presumed that they own it as tenants in common. Unlike a joint tenancy, if Jones dies, his interest passes under his will, and if he dies without a will, his interest goes to his heirs. Fox owns no more interest than he owned when Jones was alive. A chief characteristic of tenancy in common is that the deceased owner's interest passes as a part of his estate.

If two persons buy property (each owning 50%) as joint tenants with right of survivorship and not as tenants in common (or words of similar meaning showing this intent), the survivor owns the decedent's 50% interest at the death of the other. Their express agreement by putting it into joint tenancy shows that they intend for the survivor to take all. But in the absence of this agreement, it is felt that the ultimate ownership of property should not be determined by the chance of survival.

Many states have laws about these presumptions. The majority of these laws provide that if parties buy property, it shall not be presumed that they own it with right of survivorship. In California and most other states the right of survivorship is possible, but it must be clearly shown that the parties intended a joint tenancy.

The simplicity of survivorship through joint tenancy has always appealed to people, and joint tenancy is available today under California law. Although it is not correct to say that property should never be held in survivorship form, neither is it correct to say that all property should be held in survivorship form in order to save time, money, and possible litigation at an owner's death.

Problems in Community Property States

California is a community property state; as a result certain problems exist here based on the common law form of survivorship in holding and owning community property. Those who know only the laws of the common law states (as distinguished from the eight community property states which adopted the Spanish-Mexican law as the basis of marital property rights) frequently overlook the community property aspect of the problem in their writings and advice to California husbands and wives.

A review of some of the litigation involving disputes between family and nonfamily members over the ownership of property held in survivorship form best illustrates the advantages and shortcomings of holding property in joint tenancy.

Government Bonds

Frequently U.S. Bonds are registered in two or more names. A common method for a husband and wife to register such bonds is "John Doe or Mary Doe." A problem often arises if John or Mary Doe dies. Does half the interest in these bonds pass under the decedent's will or belong to the survivor named on the bond? After conflicting court rulings in several states, the U.S. Supreme Court held in 1962 that the survivor named on the bond became the sole owner at the death of the other co-owner. In the case, a husband and wife bought with community funds bonds which were valued at $87,035.50 when the wife died. In her will, she gave her share of the community property to her son. In a suit between the husband and the son to determine whether the mother's will affected the bonds, the United States Supreme Court held that the bonds belonged solely to the surviving husband because the high court held that a United States Treasury Regulation provided for the survivor to become the sole owner upon the death of a co-owner and that was superior to California law. The U.S. Supreme Court decision reversed a California Supreme Court decision which had given the surviving son half of the value of the bonds. The United States Supreme Court recognized that there is a possibility that a California spouse can commit fraud upon the other spouse by placing community funds in an "or" form registration. However, to prove fraud, the surviving spouse must sue.

The situation where this can arise is shown in a case involving alleged fraud. The husband had purchased $18,000 worth of U.S. Bonds and had registered them in his name and the name of his daughter from a prior marriage. Upon his death, under the Treasury Regulations the daughter claimed the ownership of all the bonds. In a suit seeking half the value of the bonds, the widow claimed that her husband had used community funds to purchase the bonds, thus transferring her share of the community funds to his daughter. But the wife failed to prove that the husband used community funds to buy the bonds, and she lost her case.

When a U.S. Savings Bond is registered in the name of two individuals as co-owners, either may redeem it without the other's permission. Upon the death of one, the surviving co-owner becomes the sole owner. If a bond is registered "Richard Brown, payable on death to Richard Brown, Jr.," then upon the death of Richard Brown, Richard Brown, Jr., becomes the sole owner. The bonds are not a part of the probate estate of the first to die and are not liable for payment of the decedent's debts. However, this form of registration should not be used if the person who furnishes the purchase money wants to leave the bonds to someone in his will other than the registered co-owner.

Contrary to what many believe, there is not an estate tax savings in using this form of registration. If the bonds were purchased with community funds and registered "husband or wife," half the value of the bonds would be included in the gross estate for estate tax purposes of the first spouse to die. The surviving spouse, as a named co-owner, becomes the sole owner of the bonds. Because of joint tenancy the bonds are not part of the probate estate of the deceased spouse. If the bonds are owned by only the surviving spouse at death, then the bonds will be included in the survivor's gross estate at full value and will be part of the survivor's probate estate as well.

Bank Accounts

Many lawsuits concerning survivorship provisions have involved the ownership of money in the bank at the death of one of those authorized to sign checks on a checking account or make withdrawals on a savings account. The decisions indicate failure on the part of many to distinguish and understand the difference between an agency account and a survivorship account. To avoid confusion the term *joint account* should not be used. This is a popular term, but it is misleading. The terms *convenience account* (also called *agency account* or *authorization account*) and *survivorship account* should be used to distinguish clearly between the two different types of accounts held in the names of two or more persons in a bank or savings and loan association.

A person likely to have a bank account on which two or more are authorized to sign checks is an elderly widow who lives alone. She wants to authorize someone to sign checks to pay her bills. She authorizes someone else—a son or daughter, a bookkeeper, a nurse, or the next-door-neighbor—to sign checks on her account. The question that must be determined is whether she wants the third person to own the balance on her death. If so, she asks for a signature card, signed by both, which contains the express provision ''as joint tenants with right of survivorship and not as tenants in common.'' This clearly indicates that the elderly widow wants the third party to have the funds in her account at her death. This is a simple substitute for a provision in her will.

However, if the widow wants the third party to only sign checks, she asks for an *authorization* or *agency* or *convenience* card. Not all banks or savings and loan companies will open a *convenience* account. It is inadvisable to rely solely upon what a bank teller might advise respecting the legal results of a two-party account. The rules on the subject are technical and the opening of such an account should be discussed with your lawyer. If the widow in our example has no intent to pass ownership of the balance to the third party, she may open a convenience account. The balance then is a part of her probate estate at her death. The point is that there is nothing objectionable to the widow's giving the balance to the third party friend who is assisting her in her business matters, but the problem comes after the widow's death when the question arises: "Did the widow intend that this friend own what was left in the bank?" One simple solution that avoids probate, permits the friend to take care of her, and lets the widow decide who receives the account on her death is the revocable living trust discussed in Chapter 10.

Several California cases illustrate the problems of joint accounts. In one, a woman who owned a bank account signed a signature card with a third party who was no relation to her. The card provided that ". . . the funds are to be owned jointly, with right of survivorship. . . ." The woman's will provided that the checking account in this particular bank go to her three brothers. At her death it was held that the third party owned the balance in the account because of the survivorship agreement printed on the card.

Another case involved a daughter who was permitted to write checks on her mother's account. At the mother's death, the daughter claimed the bank balance as hers because of the survivorship provision in the signature card. In a suit filed by the other sisters, it was proved that the mother had made a mistake in signing this particular card. She had intended a convenience account, not a survivorship account. However, other cases with seemingly similar facts have been decided otherwise. A brief consultation with your lawyer can avoid the significant expense of a subsequent suit.

The courts have said that the balance of separate property of a spouse held in the names of the husband and wife with right of survivorship will pass to the surviving spouse at the death of the other.

Points relevant to joint bank accounts are also applicable to owning shares of stock registered in two or more names.

Summary

Ownership of property with another person can reduce your complete control over the property. Because you are sharing ownership, under the law you will also share management and control of the property. This may not be a problem if the owners are harmonious, but the family picture can change through a divorce or a family squabble. There are no tax advantages in owning property in joint tenancy, but there can be tax disadvantages. Some property owners believe that if they place their property in a survivorship form, it will not be subject to death tax. This, however, is not so. Moreover, joint tenancy between spouses may subject property to estate tax on the death of the surviving spouse that could have avoided tax in a bypass trust. (See Chapter 13.) Under certain situations, when valuable property is transferred into survivorship form, gift tax liability may result. But sometimes the advantages of this feature are outweighed by the disadvantages. Before placing substantial amounts of property in joint tenancy form, you should clearly understand *all* the effects of sharing ownership of your property prior to your death and fully discuss the alternatives explained in the other chapters so that the most economical and efficient mechanism of meeting your objectives will be selected.

19
What Is Community Property?

The California community property system is derived from the Spanish-Mexican law in effect in California when it was acquired by the United States. The system is based on a theory that a husband and wife form a "community" and that property acquired during the existence of the community belongs equally to both spouses. Although some of the fifty states have adopted certain aspects of community property law, only eight states currently have a fully developed community property system. In addition to California, these states are Louisiana, Texas, New Mexico, Arizona, Nevada, Washington, and Idaho. Although a common basis underlies the community property systems of these eight states, important differences exist from one state to another. California's community property system is unique in many ways.

Definition of Community Property

All property acquired by either spouse during marriage while domiciled in California, other than separate property, is community property. In order to determine what is community property, one must first identify what is separate property.

Separate property is owned only by the acquiring spouse. Examples of separate property follow:

1. All property acquired by either spouse before marriage or after a judgment decreeing legal separation or divorce.
2. Property acquired by a spouse by gift or inheritance.
3. The earnings and accumulations of either spouse while living separate and apart from the other spouse.

4. Damages recovered by either spouse for personal injuries inflicted by the other spouse and recoveries for injuries inflicted by a third person if the cause of action for the recovery arose while the spouses were living separate from each other.
5. Income (technically called rents, issues, and profits) derived from the spouse's separate property.
6. Property received in exchange for or acquired with the spouse's separate property.
7. Any property which would otherwise be community property if the spouses agree before or during the marriage to treat such property as the separate property of one spouse or the other.

Status of Property as Governed by Presumptions

Where the source of any particular item of property is unclear, its characterization as separate or community property may be determined by certain legal presumptions. Most of these presumptions are not conclusive and may be rebutted by evidence to the contrary. However, they often have a significant effect on the outcome of litigation because they shift the burden of proof from one party to the other on the issue of ownership or characterization of the property as separate or community. It is therefore important to retain complete records. The following discussion outlines these important presumptions.

General Presumption of Community Property

There is a general presumption that all property acquired by either spouse during marriage is community property. Without sufficient evidence to the contrary, this presumption generally controls the characterization of property in unclear cases. There are other presumptions, however, which are discussed in the following sections.

Presumptions with Respect to Married Women

Property acquired by a married woman in her own name prior to 1975 is presumed to be her separate property. For transactions after January 1, 1975, no special presumption governs acquisitions of property by married women. Since 1975, husbands and wives have been treated equally under the laws governing presumptions.

Status of Property as Determined by Condition of Title

In general, a presumption applies that title to property indicates whether it is separate or community. However, the condition of title is *not* conclusive. Title to property may be taken in the name of either the husband or wife alone, or any recognized estate or cotenancy, and may still be shown to be community property. Either spouse or any interested party (heirs, creditors, or others) may show that notwithstanding the status of title, the spouses actually intended to hold property as community property. Such intent may be established by evidence that the spouses took title otherwise for a special reason, such as for purposes of convenience, or in the mistaken belief of the legal consequences of their actions, or even for purposes of defrauding creditors. Thus, where community property funds are used to purchase property, title to which is taken in the name of either spouse ("as his/her sole and separate property"), it may still be found that the property is a community asset.

As we discussed in the last chapter, a number of problems have arisen from the common use of the joint tenancy form by married persons in taking title to property (e.g., to John Doe and Martha Doe, husband and wife, as joint tenants), particularly where the property is acquired with community funds. California law provides that when a single-family residence of a husband and wife is acquired during marriage as joint tenants, the residence is presumed to be community property for purposes of dividing the residence in separation or marital dissolution proceedings (but may be joint tenancy property for purposes of passing title upon the death of a spouse). This presumption applies only to a single-family residence and not to the other real or personal property.

Commingling

You may endanger your separate property by commingling it with community assets. If the commingling of separate and community funds or assets is such that the identity of the separate property can no longer be traced, the entire fund or property acquired will be treated as community property under the general presumption that property acquired during marriage is community property. For example, if a husband deposits his community property earnings in the bank account in which he also deposits dividends from separate property stocks so that deposits and withdrawals from this account result in a commingling and the separate deposits can no longer be identified, the whole account will be presumed to be community property. In addition, any assets acquired by purchase through funds withdrawn from the account will be considered community property.

In attempting to trace the source of funds in an account used to purchase a particular asset, there is a presumption that community funds are used to pay community expenses. Only when all of the community funds have been exhausted are separate funds then deemed to have been used to pay such expenses. Separate funds so used are presumed to be a gift to the community unless the spouses have previously agreed to reimburse the separate property used for community purposes.

Agreements to Change the Character of Property

You have the right under California law to modify the usual community property rules through the use of agreements entered into before or during marriage. Although oral agreements may be valid in certain instances, written agreements between you and your spouse are preferable.

Such agreements are subject to certain restrictions. For example, a provision denying the right to spousal support during marriage would be invalid. Spousal agreements must also be fundamentally fair. Both spouses must freely consent to the agreement. An agreement can be invalidated where one spouse obtains the other spouse's consent through fraud, threats, undue influence, trickery, or other similar means.

Management and Control of Community Property

Subject to the limitations discussed below, both spouses have equal rights in the management and control of most community property assets. Thus, both spouses generally have management and control of the community property with the same power of disposition as either spouse has over his or her separate property. Theoretically, each spouse even has the right to manage and control the earnings of the other. However, each spouse must act in good faith with respect to the other in the management and control of any community property. One spouse cannot make a gift of community personal property without the other's consent, nor may one spouse sell, encumber, or convey the community household furniture, furnishings, or the clothing of the other without the other's written consent. Certain restrictions also are imposed with respect to the transfer, lease, or mortgage of community real property.

An exception to the "equal management" rule exists to allow each spouse who is operating or managing a business (or interest in a business) which is community personal property to have the *sole* management and control of that business (or appropriate interest therein). Examples of such businesses include the professional practices of lawyers and physicians, retail stores, and small manufacturing or wholesaling enterprises.

Management, Skill, or Efforts of One Spouse to Improve Separate Property

If you invest your separate property in a business and devote your skills during marriage to running that business, the resulting business profits will be partially community property and partially your separate property. California courts apply one of two basic rules in apportioning the profits between community and separate property depending on whether the profits are due primarily to your skill and efforts or to the natural growth from your capital investment.

Liability for Debts

Subject to certain limitations, the modern California rule is that community assets may be taken in satisfaction of any contractual liability incurred by either spouse before or during marriage. The rationale for this rule is that both spouses now have equal rights to management and control of community assets, so it follows that such assets over which they have control should be liable for their debts whenever and for whatever purposes those debts were incurred. Since community assets may generally be used to satisfy any liability incurred by either spouse prior to or during marriage, you cannot insulate yourself from liability for existing debts by getting married. However, there is a major exception to this rule: the earnings of a spouse during marriage (although community property) are not subject to liability for debts incurred by the other spouse prior to marriage.

Where community assets are used to pay off a premarital debt owed by one spouse, a court may order reimbursement to the community in the event of a subsequent marital dissolution. For instance, in one case where a husband used community assets of a subsequent marriage to pay alimony and child support to his former wife, a California Appellate Court ordered that the husband "reimburse" the community out of his separate property assets.

Different rules govern the liability of community property for the death or injury to persons or property caused by one or both of the spouses. Community property may be used to pay such liabilities, but under certain circumstances, the separate property of the spouse who caused the death or injury must be used to make such payments before any community property may be used.

Community Property upon the Death of a Spouse

In California, you have the power to give by will your one half of the community property as well as your entire separate property. A decedent, either a husband or wife, may even attempt to dispose of the entire community property by forcing the surviving spouse to make an election as explained in our discussion of the widow's election in Chapter 13.

If you do not leave a valid will (i.e. you die "intestate"), your share of the community property passes to your surviving spouse.

Quasi-Community Property

California law provides for what is known as *quasi-community property*. This kind of property is designed to treat residents of common law states who move to California after marriage as if they had been domiciled in California throughout their marriage to the extent permitted by constitutional principles. For purposes of determining the passage of property upon the death of a spouse, quasi-community property is personal property, wherever situated, and real property situated in California which either (a) was acquired by the decedent while domiciled elsewhere and would have been community property if the decedent had been domiciled in California at the time of its acquisition; or (b) was acquired in exchange for real or personal property, wherever situated, which would have been community property if the decedent had been domiciled in California at the time the property so exchanged was acquired.

Out-of-state land is excluded from the quasi-community property definition for purposes of determining to whom the property will pass upon the death of a spouse, although it is included for purposes of dividing the spouses' property in a marital dissolution and legal separation.

Unlike true community property, the non-owner spouse has no actual, vested interest in quasi-community property during the owner's lifetime. Thus, the non-owner spouse cannot dispose of such property by will if he or she predeceases the owner spouse. However, when the owner spouse dies first, the quasi-community property is treated like true community property, and the non-owner spouse has the right to one half. But prior to 1985, the non-owner spouse may have to renounce any interest as beneficiary under the owner spouse's will in order to exercise this right. You should consult an attorney about the final effects of changes in California law concerning quasi-community property after January 1, 1985.

Illustration of the Need for Careful Planning

A recent California Appellate Court decision illustrates the need for careful planning with community property in the context of probate. John Doe and Mary Doe were married early in 1974. John Doe was a widower, and Mary Doe was a widow. Both had children from their prior marriages, all of whom were adults at the time John and Mary were married. In 1975, John and Mary purchased a home taking title as joint tenants. John died in 1977. His will made reference to the new home and declared it to be the community property of John and Mary with title being held in joint tenancy form for convenience only. The will also named John's son and daughter as beneficiaries. John's son filed a petition in the Probate Court seeking to have the home declared the community property of John and Mary. During the court proceedings, testimony was offered that John wanted the home to be considered community property so that he could give his one-half interest in the home to his children as their inheritance, but in the event that Mary predeceased John, title to the home would vest in John without a lengthy Probate Court proceeding. Mary testified that John had never discussed the actual character of the home as either separate or community property and he had simply told her that she would receive the home upon his death.

The Court of Appeal held that for purposes of determining to whom property passes upon the death of a spouse, there is a presumption that the character of real property, whether or not a personal residence, is as set forth in the deed. Since there was no agreement between John and Mary that the house was community property, the joint tenancy title passed the house to Mary.

Thus, the court determined that John and Mary had not agreed to hold the house as community property and that title to the house should pass to Mary as the surviving joint tenant. Underlying the court's decision was a strong disapproval of John's "hidden intent" to make sure he would have a share of the residence whether or not he survived Mary. John's attempts to "hedge his bets" and manipulate the community property law to his benefit resulted in the frustration of his desires and the disinheritance of his children.

20
My Farm or Business

Many people have devoted their lives and energies to developing a successful business enterprise. It may be a sole proprietorship, a partnership, or a closely held corporation. The type of business involved may include anything from farming to manufacturing. It may employ 2 persons or 2,000. Whether the success resulting from the individual who was the spark behind the business can survive his death will depend largely upon the amount of planning that has been done for the protection of the business.

Most businessmen are so preoccupied with daily business problems that they fail to realize that all the benefits of their business may be lost to their family after their death, unless proper preparations have been made for the orderly continuation or disposition of these business interests.

Failure to recognize, analyze, and solve these special estate planning problems may lead to a forced sale or other deleterious disposition of your family farm or business at a time when your family is least able to absorb the loss.

What are some of the basic problems which should be considered in planning to protect the value of a farm or business at the time of the owner's death?

Sale or Continued Operation

The first consideration is whether to sell the business or continue its operation. This important decision will provide the framework for planning the protection of your family.

Any business can become paralyzed following the death of its owner. Uninterrupted production during this period is usually difficult because the individual who has been responsible for the daily operations and decisions is gone. An orderly plan for the immediate transfer of operational and managerial control or sale is essential.

In a sole proprietorship you usually own all of the assets of the business yourself. Upon your death, your executor may wish to liquidate the business without delay to avoid personal liability for failing to run it properly unless he has been relieved of this liability by express provision in the will.

If the primary income producing factor is your personal services, it is probably advisable to plan for a sale of the business assets to take place at your death. Care should be exercised in specifying which assets used in the business are to be sold, and some specific provisions should be made for payment of business liabilities. To facilitate this sale, any leases of business assets should be made assumable and debts either covered by life insurance or not subject to acceleration. You should solve any problems in the transferability of your business assets while you are alive and should consult counsel for guidance to avoid any hidden surprises that will hamper the sale of the business by your family.

If the business is one in which your capital investment was the primary income producing factor, it may be in the best interests of your family to arrange for a continuation of the business. This may be done by directing your executor to continue the business and by providing him with broad powers in your will to permit prompt action in exercising sound business judgment. The will may determine the form of the business, it may direct that the business be incorporated, and it may provide for an immediate transfer and delivery of the business assets to insure continuity of operations. The assets must be reviewed when the will is prepared to be sure they will be easily transferrable with any consents from lenders or leasors readily obtainable.

A partnership is dissolved on the death of a partner unless otherwise provided in the partnership agreement. The surviving partners may have to liquidate the business and make an accounting to the deceased partner's estate. It is possible by making appropriate provisions in the partnership agreement to continue partnership operations with the decedent's estate or beneficiaries or to buy them out. The deceased partner's will should coordinate with the provisions in the partnership agreement.

Partnership agreements can be drawn to protect the deceased partner's interest from forced sale or involuntary liquidation. The partners should decide during their lifetimes whether to sell their interests at death or to provide for the continued participation of their surviving families. This decision should be incorporated into the partnership agreement and each partner's will in order to protect both the surviving partner, or partners, and the decedent's family.

The decision to sell or continue to operate a decedent's corporation is complex. The general considerations we discussed in selling a sole proprietorship are equally applicable here. If personal services are a major factor, a sale at death is desirable, while the business may be continued if capital investment is the major factor. In addition, it is necessary to consider other factors.

The ownership of a corporate business is evidenced by the stock certificate. Your stock ownership may represent a substantial part of your estate. The problems this creates are probably best resolved in light of the existing business conditions at the time of your death. Hence, your executor should be given discretionary powers to participate in the management and operations of the corporation. The executor of a will or a trustee of either a testamentary trust or a living trust may be given specific instructions as to how and when to sell the stock, to whom to sell it, and when and under what circumstances it should be sold. If you give these directions in light of your experience and judgment in the business operations, they will provide valuable guidelines to protect the business after your death.

Liquidity

Death creates a need for cash. Many businessmen operate on credit for extensive periods of time and are constantly rearranging their business financing to provide working capital for their personal needs. This source of cash usually ends upon death. Yet funds must be provided for the family's living expenses, as well as for debts and various taxes.

If the business or its assets are to be sold, the terms of the sale should be structured to insure the availability of funds for debts and taxes. If the business is to be continued at death, you must plan the availability of sufficient funds for debts and taxes to make sure the business can continue and does not have to be sold.

With a sole proprietorship cash may be generated from the sale of specific assets, the maintenance of life insurance, or the borrowing of necessary funds by your executor with appropriate directions and powers in your will.

In a partnership where the partners have so agreed, taxes may be paid with withdrawals from the deceased partner's capital account. Current partnership earnings may also be available for a period after death for this purpose. It is important to designate these payments as a continuation of income participation by the deceased partner's estate so that such payments are not mistaken for payments in purchase of the decedent's interest. The partners should plan in advance to finance the purchase of a decedent's interest as well as the continued operations during this difficult transition period.

Special Corporate Redemption

Naturally, the owners of a closely held corporation may experience great difficulty in raising cash because of the limited market for their securities. However, under certain conditions the law permits a corporation to redeem a decedent's stock to fund funeral expenses, death taxes, and other costs of administering the decedent's estate. The corporation may provide the needed cash from accumulated earnings without adverse income tax consequences to the decedent's estate if the redemption price of the stock is equal to its estate tax value.

To qualify for this income tax benefit, the value of the decedent's stock in the closely held corporation must exceed 35% of the decedent's adjusted gross estate. The adjusted gross estate is generally the gross estate minus the debts, losses, and funeral and administrative expenses. Stock in two or more businesses may be aggregated together to exceed this 35% requirement if a decedent owned 20% or more of the value in each such business.

The redemption may be made for cash, a promissory note or other corporate property. Moreover, the funds or property withdrawn need not be actually used to pay the death tax, funeral, and administrative expenses.

Installment Payment of a Portion of the Federal Estate Tax

The estate may also qualify for an installment payment of that portion of the federal estate tax attributable to a closely held business. The estate may pay interest only for five years followed by ten annual installments of principal and interest. Interest on the deferred estate tax on the first one million dollars in value of the business is 4%, and interest on the balance of the deferred tax is paid at the then-current interest rate for tax deficiencies. However, the increasing unified credit, discussed in Chapter 11, will reduce the "4% portion" of the estate tax as follows:

1983	$266,500
1984	$249,500
1985	$224,000
1986	$190,000
1987	$153,000

Generally most businesses will qualify; however, certain kinds of activities such as management of passive investments will not. The requirement for qualification should be carefully reviewed with counsel.

In addition, the decedent's interest in the closely held business must exceed 35% of the adjusted gross estate, but two or more business interests can be combined to exceed this 35% requirement if the decedent owned 20% or more of the total value of each such business.

After a family begins the installment payments, there are still some concerns. Acceleration of the unpaid federal estate tax can occur if more than 50% of the business is sold or withdrawn during the installment period. Failure to pay either the interest or principal on any installment may also trigger acceleration.

Special Use Valuation for Farms and Real Property Used in a Trade or Business

Property is valued at its "highest and best use" for purposes of assessing the federal estate tax. A relief provision is available in view of the inequity of valuing land used for farming or in a business at its "highest and best use" when the income it produces may be insufficient to pay the tax. The executor may elect to have this real estate valued on the basis of its actual use in the farm or business.

This real property must be included in the decedent's gross estate and must be "qualified real property" applied to a "qualified use" that passes to a "qualified heir." Proper planning is critical to enjoy this valuable relief provision.

A maximum reduction in valuation of $750,000 from the "highest and best use" value is allowed.

Buy-Sell Agreements

In planning it is important to accommodate the potential dynamic between the needs of the surviving family for cash to settle the estate and maintain their standard of living and the needs of the business for cash for operations. Our discussion now turns to one of the solutions—the buy-sell agreement.

This agreement is a contract which provides for the purchase and sale of the business interest, whether a sole proprietorship, partnership, or corporation. The contract is used to protect the surviving family from forced sales and depressed prices while protecting the continuing owners or operators of the business from the interference of those in the decedent's family who are not active in the business.

Buy-sell agreements may include provisions for funding the purchase price and assuring that the cash will be available to the decedent's estate. These provisions may be as broad and varied as the imagination of the business planner.

Parties to a buy-sell agreement may be found both in and out of the business. The sole proprietor may look to certain key employees who may be interested in taking over the farm or business. The same considerations would apply to one who is the only shareholder of a closely held corporation. Where there is more than one owner, the other owners may agree to purchase the decedent's interest. A competitor may also be interested in participating in a buy-sell agreement.

You should structure the sale of your business while you are alive when your family's bargaining position is greater. A properly drafted buy-sell agreement will also fix the value of the stock for federal estate tax purposes and thereby make planning for those cash needs easier. We will now discuss the various types of buy-sell agreements.

The "Option" or "Right of First Refusal" Agreement

The most flexible of these agreements is the *option* or *right of first refusal*. The business owner still has the opportunity to sell at a higher price if the holders of the option or right of first refusal fail to buy. Since they are not bound to purchase the business, they may re-assess their personal circumstances before they exercise their option or right of first refusal. Their freedom not to buy creates uncertainty for the deceased owner's estate. These agreements, therefore, do not meet the several tests for creating a binding value for federal estate tax purposes.

The Cross-Purchase Agreement

By contrast the cross-purchase agreement obligates the estate of a deceased owner to sell to the remaining owners who in turn are obligated to purchase the decedent's interest from the estate. The parties to this agreement are the individual owners and not the partnership or corporation itself.

The cross-purchase agreement permits the surviving owners to obtain a higher income tax basis for their share of the business because the cost of purchasing the decedent's share is included in that tax basis.

However, the cross-purchase agreement presents some problems. First, the surviving owners may find it very difficult to personally raise the funds necessary to purchase the decedent's interest. An installment sale can alleviate this problem to some extent. Life insurance policies which pay proceeds to the surviving owners on the decedent's death are also an alternative, but each business owner must maintain a life insurance policy on the life of each other owner.

The Redemption Agreement

Many businesses therefore select the "entity purchase" or "redemption" agreement where the business entity (partnership or closely held corporation) agrees to purchase the interest of a retiring or deceased owner. Corporate funds can be used to purchase the interest of the decedent. A corporate redemption can be funded through life insurance with only one policy needed on the life of each owner in contrast to the multiplicity of policies required in the cross-purchase agreement.

If certain conditions are met, a corporation may use its own appreciated assets to redeem the interest of a deceased owner without recognizing taxable gain (other than depreciation recapture).

With careful planning dividend treatment may be avoided on the redemption proceeds received by the estate.

Similar considerations with some differences apply to a partnership buy-sell agreement. The interest of a former partner can be purchased through a cross-purchase agreement or may be liquidated by the partnership itself.

Community Property

As we discussed in the last chapter, California is a community property state. It should be remembered that if all or even a part of the business is community property, the death of either spouse may create financial problems, since each owns one half of the community property.

Therefore, it is necessary to consider the generalizations we discussed in this chapter as they relate to the financial needs of the husband upon the wife's death and vice versa. Failure to recognize that the death of either spouse in a community property state can create severe cash problems may produce serious consequences.

Each businessperson should see that his or her spouse's share of the community property is protected in the event the spouse dies first. This will involve having the spouse's estate planned following the same basic program designed to protect the value of the business should the businessperson die first. It should be noted that while the unlimited marital deduction may mitigate the estate tax liability, its selective use for certain assets is required to achieve optimum estate planning.

Summary

There are no cure-all substitutes for thorough business planning to preserve the value of a farm or business at the owner's death. Nor is there a single device by which all problems created at death can be easily resolved.

A well considered plan which studies each of the problems peculiar to the business operation of the individual is essential to preserve and protect the value of the business at death.

Glossary

Adjusted gross estate: used only for federal estate tax purposes. The adjusted gross estate is the value of the decedent's estate for federal tax purposes figured by subtracting funeral and administrative expenses, debts, taxes, and certain other items from the total value of the estate.

Administrator: one appointed by the court to administer the estate of the decedent. His principal duties are to collect the properties of the estate, pay the debts of the decedent, and distribute the estate to the people entitled to it. An administrator is appointed if the decedent failed to nominate an executor in his will or died without a will. The feminine form of adminstrator is "administratrix."

Appreciation: growth in the fair market value of the property. The term usually refers to an increase due to fluctuation in the market value of the property rather than changes in the property itself. Antonym: depreciation.

Beneficiary: one for whose benefit a trust is created, or one to whom the proceeds of insurance are payable.

Commingling: the placing together of property of various kinds. In California the term has special significance with respect to community property and refers to the mixing of one spouse's separate property with community property or with separate property of the other spouse.

Community property: property acquired by either spouse during marriage, except by gift, will or inheritance. This is a property system based on the theory that marriage is a partnership. California is one of eight community property states.

Convenience account: a bank account established by one person in the name of himself and another person for the purpose of allowing either person to draw out money to be used for the benefit of the first person. A common example of a convenience account is where the first person is aged or ill and is unable to go to the bank to obtain funds. The account is established to allow the second person to draw funds for the "convenience" of the first.

Court-made law: law which is established by court decision rather than by the act of the legislature. This term applies to interpretations of statutes and theories set forth in court decisions.

Decedent: a deceased person. The term refers either to one who dies leaving a will or to one who dies without a will.

Devise: (noun) a gift of real estate which is made by the will of a deceased person; (verb) to give real estate by means of a will. Note: After January 1, 1985, a devise will include personal property also.

Devisee: one who receives real estate under the terms of a will. Note: After January 1, 1985, a devisee will include one who receives personal property also.

Disposition: transmitting or directing property ownership, as in disposition of property by a person's will.

Encumbrance: a claim, lien, charge, or liability against property, such as a mortgage.

Estate: the entire property owned by a person, whether land or moveable property. In the probate context, however, the term refers to only that property left by a decedent that is administered by the personal representative subject to the control of the court.

Executor: one who is appointed under the will of a decedent to manage the estate and to carry out the directions in the will for disposition of the estate property. The feminine of executor is "executrix."

Fair market value: the value of property that would be set by an owner willing (but not forced) to sell and a buyer willing (but not forced) to buy, with both buyer and seller knowing all relevant facts. The fair market value of property is intended to be an estimate of value which is fair, economic, and reasonable under normal conditions.

Grantor: a person who transfers property to someone else (known as the "grantee" or if in trust known as the "trustee"). The term is generally used to describe the one who transfers property by gift or by sale.

Holographic will: a will written in the handwriting of the testator.

Intestate: a person is said to die intestate when he leaves no valid will to control the disposition of his property.

Joinder: joining or coupling together, uniting with another person in some legal step or proceeding.

Joint tenancy with right of survivorship: generally, ownership of property by two or more persons who have the same interest in the property and own it together; all rights in the property pass to the survivor(s) upon the death of any one joint tenant and ultimately pass to the last survivor. Thus, the interest of a joint tenant is not included in his probate estate when he dies.

Letters testamentary: a document of authority issued to an executor by the probate court showing his authority to serve as executor.

Liquidity: used to describe whether an asset can be converted into cash easily. For example, stock that can be easily sold has good liquidity; stock that cannot be easily sold has poor liquidity.

Personalty: property other than real estate is said to be "personalty." The term also applies to contract rights.

Posting: giving public notice, generally by displaying a written announcement in an official, conspicuous place, such as attaching a notice to the courthouse bulletin board.

Probate: the court procedure that includes proving to the satisfaction of the probate court that an instrument is the last will and testament of the decedent.

Quitclaim deed: the deed intended to transfer whatever interest the grantor had, if he had any at all. This deed is distinguished from a grant deed, in which the grantor guarantees that he does have a certain interest.

Realty: land and mineral interests. This includes buildings located on the land. Synonyms: real estate, real property, or immoveables.

Self-proving will: a will that does not require that the witnesses do anything further to prove that an uncontested will was properly signed by the testator, because the witnesses signed an attestation clause under penalty of perjury that the will was correctly signed.

Separate property: property owned by either spouse before marriage or property received by gift, under a will, or through inheritance during marriage.

Survivorship account: a bank account in the name of two or more persons in which the entire amount passes to the survivor or survivors upon the death of one of the owners. The account may be with a company other than a bank.

Tenants in common: ownership by two or more persons of the same piece of property in which each has the right to use and occupy the property at the same time with all the other owners. This type of ownership differs from the "joint tenancy with right of survivorship," in that the interest of the deceased owner does not automatically pass to the survivors. Thus, a tenant in common may dispose of his interest by will.

Testator: one who has made a will; one who dies leaving a will. The feminine of testator is "testatrix."

Trust: a legal arrangement in which property is held by one person as a fiduciary for the benefit of another person.

Trustee: the person who holds the property in trust for the benefit of the other person who is called the beneficiary.

Valuation: the act of ascertaining or estimating the worth of property.

About the Authors

Kathryn A. Ballsun, A.B., 1968, University of Southern California; J.D., 1976, Loyola University. Ms. Ballsun is a partner in the firm of Stanton and Ballsun and has taught for the California Continuing Education of the Bar, University of California, Los Angeles, Clinical Program; the University of Southern California; and for Loyola University on estate administration and planning. She is a member of the Beverly Hills Bar Association, Board of Governors, 1982–1984, and was chairman of the Probate, Trust and Estate Planning Section, 1980–1982. She also contributed to the *Beverly Hills Bar Association Journal,* Vol. II, No. 4 (July–August, 1977).

Regina Covitt, B.A., 1973, University of Massachusetts; M.A., 1976, and J.D., 1981, University of California, Los Angeles. Ms. Covitt is an associate with the firm of Irell & Manella and is a member of the Beverly Hills Bar Association Probate, Trust and Estate Planning Section.

Kenneth A. Feinfield, B.A., 1966, University of California, Los Angeles; J.D. (with honors), 1972, University of San Fernando Valley. Mr. Feinfield is a member of the firm of Antin, Stern, Litz & Grebow, Los Angeles, and is vice-chairman of the Beverly Hills Bar Association Probate, Trust and Estate Planning Section, 1983–1984. He is a frequent speaker on various probate and estate planning topics before attorney, accountant, and real estate broker groups and was a panelist and co-author of "Probate, Trust and Estate Planning Developments" for the Beverly Hills Bar Association, Third Annual Update of the Law Program (1983).

Douglas K. Freeman, A.B. (with distinction), 1967, Stanford University; J.D., 1970, University of California, Los Angeles; LL.M., Tax, University of San Diego, 1984. A certified specialist in taxation, Mr. Freeman is a principal in the firm of Freeman, Freeman & Smiley, specializing in tax, pension, professional corporations, and estate planning. He was an instructor of law, U.S. Air Force, 1973–1975; co-chairman, Symposium on New Thrusts in Estate Planning: Capital Freeze Techniques, University of Southern California, 1980; and Chairman, Conference on Estate Freezing, Georgetown Law Center, and University of California, Berkeley, May 1981. He is a frequent lecturer for the California Continuing Education of the Bar. His publications include *Estate Freezing: Tools and Techniques; Fundamentals of California Probate,* co-authored with Arthur Bowman, 1976; and "The Charitable Partner in Estate Planning," *Trusts and Estates* (Fall 1981).

Jonathan A. Karp, B.S. (Phi Beta Kappa with highest honors), 1973, University of California, Berkeley; J.D., 1976, University of Michigan. Mr. Karp is a partner of the Beverly Hills firm of Burris, Karp & Mooney and is licensed as a certified public accountant in California. He is a member of the Beverly Hills Bar Association Probate, Trust and Estate Planning Section and the American Bar Association Sections of Taxation and Real Property, Probate and Trust Law. He has also lectured on estate planning and probate before the University of West Los Angeles School of Law (Continuing Education) and the Society of California Accountants, Beverly Hills Chapter.

Irving Kellog is licensed as an attorney and CPA in California and is currently of counsel for the firm of Alschuler, Grossman & Pines. He is the author of the books *How to Find Negligence and Misrepresentations in Financial Statements* and *Managing an Estate Planning Practice* and of the articles "The Importance of Wills" and "A Plan for Drafting in Plain English." He has lectured for the California Continuing Education of the Bar; University of Southern California; University of California, Los Angeles; and the California CPA Foundation.

James L. Pocrass, B.S., 1970, California State University, Northridge; J.D., 1973, Loyola University of Los Angeles; admitted to California bar, 1973. Mr. Pocrass of James L. Pocrass, A Law Corporation, is a partner of the firm Wolf, Pocrass and Reyes, and is a member of the Los Angeles County Bar Association, the Beverly Hills Bar Association, the American Bar Association, the State Bar of California, and the Association of Southern California Defense Counsel.

Victor E. Portanova, B.A., 1968, Dartmouth College; J.D., 1971, Fordham Law School; LL.M., 1972, New York University. Mr. Portanova practices with the firm of Portanova and Pensig, A Law Corporation, Beverly Hills. He has been certified as a taxation specialist by the State Bar of California. He is also an associate professor at the Golden Gate University Tax Masters Program.

Gary Mitchell Ruttenberg, B.S., 1967, University of California, Los Angeles; J.D., 1970, Loyola Law School. Mr. Ruttenberg is a member of the firm Bloom & Ruttenberg. He has been a chairman of the Beverly Hills Bar Association Probate, Trust and Estate Planning Section, 1980–1981 and authored the "Case on Point" column for the *Probate and Trust Law Section Newsletter* of the Los Angeles County Bar Association. He has also lectured for the California Continuing Education of the Bar on fundamentals of estate administration (1981 and 1982).

Nina Madden Sabban, B.A., 1965, University of California, Los Angeles; J.D., 1978, Loyola Law School. Ms. Sabban is a member of the firm Hoffman, Sabban & Brucker, Beverly Hills. She is a member of the Executive Committee, Probate and Trust Section of Los Angeles County Bar, 1982. Her publications include "California's Community Property Laws: Planning for a Move to California," *Trusts and Estates,* June 1982; "Husband and Wife Property: Who Owns What?" *The California Society for Certified Public Accountants,* 1980.

Myron Siedorf, J.D., 1950, University of Southern California; LL.M., 1961, University of Southern California. Mr. Siedorf is chief counsel of the Division of Tax Administration for the California State Controller. He is a specialist in taxation and author of the practice book for the California Continuing Education of the Bar entitled *California Inheritance Tax Practice.*

Lance M. Weagant, A.B., *magna cum laude,* 1972, University of Southern California; J.D., 1976, University of Southern California; Certificate in Taxation, 1979, University of San Diego School of Law, Graduate Program in Taxation. Mr. Weagant, a State Bar certified specialist in taxation law, is a member of the firm of Fowler, Vanic, Weagant, and Loo. Mr. Weagant specializes in taxation, estate planning, and trust and probate law. He has taught estate and gift tax planning for the American College, Solomon S. Huebner School of Chartered Life Underwriting Studies, since 1980 and presented the topic of "Probate, Trust, and Estate Planning Developments" at the Beverly Hills Bar Association's Third Annual Update of the Law Program (1983). He is a member of the Beverly Hills Estate Planning Council and chaired the Legislative Subcommittee of the Beverly Hills Bar Association Probate, Trust and Estate Planning Section for 1982–1983.

The Editor

Leland Alan Stark, A.B., 1965, University of California, Los Angeles; J.D., 1972, University of California, Los Angeles. Mr. Stark practices with the law offices of Leland Alan Stark, Beverly Hills. He is currently vice-chairman of the Estate Planning and Drafting—Charitable Giving—Committee of the Real Property, Probate and Trust Law Section of the American Bar Association. He has served as a Judge Pro-Tem of the Beverly Hills and Los Angeles Municipal Courts and as an arbitrator for the American Arbitration Association. He has contributed to articles on taxation published by Prentice-Hall and the University of Southern California Tax Institute and is a frequent lecturer and panelist at universities, private seminars, and charitable organizations on estate planning and charitable giving.

Index